# FERRARI

# 308 328 348

ISBN 978-1-84155-584-3

# FERRARI CONTENTS

## ME & MY

# FERRARI 308

It looked like a scrapyard relic and would cost £6000 to fix but, to Italian car lover Richard Morley, buying a Ferrari was a challenge

| | |
|---|---|
| **Driver** | Richard J Morley, managing director |
| **Car** | 1984 Ferrari 308GTS QV |
| **Bought** | September 1991 |
| **Price** | £18,000 |
| **Private sale value today** | £25,000 |
| **Previous owners** | Five |
| **Service history when bought** | None |
| **Mileage then** | 21,000 |
| **Mileage now** | 25,800 |
| **Servicing costs** | None (see text) |
| **Days off road** | Eight months, but none since rebuild |
| **Faults** | Cracked windscreen |
| **Insurance cost** | £1500 on motor trade policy with full no-claims and clean licence (limited mileage policy £1200) |
| **DIY servicing** | All (see text) |
| **Likes** | Handling, classic looks, inspires respect, driving position, running costs equivalent to large executive saloon |
| **Dislikes** | Harshness of engine |
| **Would he recommend one?** | Yes |

THE PHONE CALL WAS brief and to the point. It concerned an Italian deal ... and made an offer that former Alfa Romeo dealer Richard Morley could not refuse.

Richard says: "I was so intrigued when I heard of a 1984-model Ferrari 308GTS going for only £18,000 that I had to go to see it."

There, at a colleague's business premises, he found a car

that looked more like scrapyard fodder than the piece of proud Italian heritage he'd expected.

"I'd been told on the phone that the car was in a state of disrepair — but it was obvious it had been subject to a heavy bout of vandalism."

Despite the amount of daunting renovation work required, Richard, with his professional experience of Italian sports cars, decided to buy the

PSU 296

Ferrari. "It represented a challenge. I had never even contemplated any work on a 308 before."

The one niggle worrying him before buying the Ferrari was its lack of service history. His friend assured him the car *really* had covered only the 21,000 miles on its clock in the hands of its five previous owners.

When he bought the 308 in September 1991, he didn't underestimate the amount of time and energy needed to bring it back to the manufacturer's specification. He reckoned the cost of the rebuild would be around £6000 and, with 1984 308s fetching upwards of £30,000 then, was sure it was worth spending that much.

During the restoration, Richard recalls, the most time-consuming job was reshaping the old panels that were still usable and fitting the new panels that were needed.

"We started from a bare-metal shell and all the work was done using a set of workshop manuals I bought for the job," says Richard. "Parts are available 24 hours a day from some suppliers, often with next-day delivery."

Richard took eight months to rebuild the Ferrari. But every minute spent doing it seemed worthwhile when the day to drive it finally dawned.

"The Ferrari 308 is one of the most exciting cars in the world — the way the power is transmitted to the road is superb, and the chassis is one of the safest, most intriguing I've ever come across," he says.

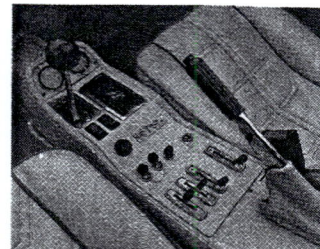

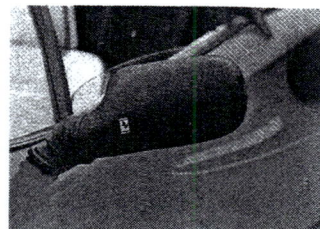

"Because of the 308's forgiving handling, you can cover vast mileages quickly, without the car biting back at all."

Since its rebuild, the 308 has had no more trouble from the more destructive members of the public. Richard says: "I believe that, while people look on an Integrale or a Cosworth as an easy, stealable target, they will just stand back from a Ferrari and admire it."

Richard's love of Italian sports cars doesn't end with his Ferrari. He held an Alfa Romeo franchise for 27 years and so he's no stranger to the design quirks of Latin machines. "People often say it's wrong to have the steering wheel so offset to the left, but the right-hand side of the body is the dominant side and, therefore, if the column is offset to the left, it makes steering easier," he says.

But isn't the 308 very expensive to run? "I've been asked that several times — it's a myth. The Ferrari name has this stigma attached to it, but I think it's wrong.

"On long runs, the 308 averages 25-27mpg. Even at worst, I've extracted 17. Any competent mechanic, with the right manuals, can service it. The only major expense can be tyres. Overall, the running costs are similar to a modern large executive saloon car."

To prove his point, Richard quotes the 308's running costs since the rebuild. "Apart from a crack in the windscreen because of shifting body panels, one-and-a-half pints of oil, and petrol — it hasn't cost me a penny," he says.

This theme runs to insurance too. "I have a motor trade association policy but, for a 35-year-old who's 'clean', with full no-claims discount, it shouldn't set you back more than £1500 a year." While that cost represents the price of a decent used car to some people, it is cheap for a Ferrari.

With an additional 4800 miles on the 308's clock, there's one small complaint — the engine's slight harshness up to 70mph. "Apart from that, I'm very happy with my investment," he says ... before revealing that he has just added a Ferrari 400i to his stable. ∎

# FERRARI DINO 308
# CHASSIS IDENTIFICATION

## October 1973

Ferrari Dino 308GT4 2+2 model announced in Italy. Replacement, though not direct replacement, for Dino 246GT models.

## May 1974

308GT4 2+2 first imported into Great Britain.
*From* .......................................................................*308GT4 2+2*      08354

## January 1975

Imports continued, but electric windows, tinted glass and heated rear
window now extra. *From* .......................................*308GT4 2+2*      08918

## May 1976

"Dino" name dropped and GT4 model now known simply as a Ferrari.
Styling changed to suit. From ...............................*308GT4 2+2*      12286
First imports of two-seater 308GTB coupé, which was a direct replacement
for the obsolete 246GT model.
With glass fibre body panels. *From*.......................*308GTB*      19149

## May 1977

Last glass-fibre bodied car imported:                                      21253
Imports of steel-bodied 308GTB began *at:* ...........*308GTB*      21333

## February 1978

First imports of 308GTS model, mechanically as 308GTB but with
detachable roof panel. *From*.................................*308GTS*      23419

*All models continue in production in 1980*

## Worried by the success of the Porsche 911, Ferrari needed a new model to replace the V6 Dino. The result was the V8 Bertone 308GT4 and the pretty Pininfarina 308GTB

THE MID-1970s were far from happy times for prestige sports car manufacturers, especially in Italy. Two shadows hung over Ferrari, Lamborghini and Maserati, the three great rivals grouped so closely in the Bologna-Modena area. One was the great energy crisis brought about by events in the Middle East, the other was Porsche.

If it was Porsche more than anything which drove Ferrari to conceive the 308, it was the energy crisis which – in a peculiar kind of way – fully justified it. Both assertions take some proving.

To understand the Porsche influence, you have to go far enough back in history to appreciate the split which developed in the 1960s between the big 12-cylinder 'proper' production Ferraris and the delicate, lightweight six-cylinder Dino, originally launched as a completely separate marque whose cars nowhere carried the Ferrari name. The Dino appeared at about the time the Porsche 911 was first establishing itself; no longer was the Stuttgart company a mere manufacturer of rebodied Volkswagens. Then, in the course of the next few years, the 911 was developed steadily in one direction: bigger engines, higher performance, better equipment. It reached the point where the 911 which had once been a Dino 246 competitor now slotted more neatly into the gap between the Dino and the V12s.

Thus, when Ferrari had to consider what should be done with the Dino after its years of production, the answer was obvious: follow Porsche up-market with a bigger car of at least nominal 2+2 layout. It was, incidentally, a decision which was reached in parallel by Lamborghini in developing the Urraco, and Maserati with the Merak.

Such a car could not be a replacement for the Dino 246 in any literal sense, even though its production stopped when that of the 308 began. Even a nominal 2+2 would need a longer wheelbase and would be a substantially bigger and heavier car. It would also need a bigger engine – too big by Ferrari's standards for a V6, no matter how far Porsche was willing to stretch its flat-six power pack. On the other hand, there was no point in going all the way to a V12 which would make the new car too expensive, quite apart from blurring the separate Dino image. In other words the new model would have to be V8-powered. This posed a problem because Ferrari was not exactly overflowing with V8 experience even though various prototype units had been made from time to time, principally for the Tipo 158 Formula One car which took the World Championship in 1964.

However, Ferrari's engine designers are

renowned for nothing if not their adaptability and speed of operation, and it did not take long for them to come up with a 90 degree V8 of nominal 3-litre capacity. From this, of course, came the 308 model designation: 3.0 litres, 8 cylinders, following the new system introduced for the Dino series. The chosen dimensions were 81 mm bore and 71 mm stroke, giving a capacity of 2927 cc. Although people normally expect Ferrari engines to sacrifice simplicity and ease of production in favour of performance, the V8 (like the Dino V6 before it) was actually designed as far as possible to ease production machining with all passes along the block, for instance, taking place either parallel or perpendicular to the cylinder head faces. Indeed, the 308 was designed to use the V6 production facilities as far as practicable.

Switching from a V6 to a V8 is a swings-and-roundabouts move for an engine designer. Assuming the V6 had an angle of 60 degrees between banks (the Dino was actually 65 degrees) then the V8 is almost bound to be lower, while offering more space between the cylinder banks to install a decent inlet manifold.

Undoubtedly the Ferrari designers welcomed the extra inlet clearance but the increased length must have worried them, the more so because it was added to by a decision to use toothed-belt drive rather than chains for the camshafts. Had the engine been in-line it would not have been such a worry, but no serious thought was given to the 308 layout following any other pattern than the Dino 246, one of a transverse mid-engine immediately aft of the cabin. The cylinders were therefore packed

> **❛ ... the original V8 produced 250 bhp ... a handsome improvement ... ❜**

close together (note also that the V8's bore/stroke ratio is less 'over-square' than in most Ferraris) even though this compelled the use of very narrow main bearings for the crankshaft. Any danger in this area was overcome by making those bearings of very large diameter, and strongly supported by the surrounding crankcase structure.

The engine had four camshafts, of course, each pair being driven by a separate toothed belt in turn driven by gears driven off the crankshaft nose. The chosen angle between the valves was 'only' 46 degrees which gave a nicely straight inlet tract but forced the exhaust to turn through a notably sharper angle downstream of its valve. This was probably a small price to pay for the com-

pactness of the whole arrangement. In line with established Ferrari practice the engine used 'wet' cast-iron liners pressed into the alloy block, directly located against each other by machined flats on their flanges.

Breathing through four twin-choke Weber 40DCNF carburettors, and with a compression ratio of 8.8:1, the original V8 produced 250 bhp at 7700 rpm, a handsome improvement over the 195 bhp of the V6 Dino. Just as useful was the rise in torque from 166 lb ft to 210 lb ft at 5000 rpm: vital, indeed, in view of the new model's greater weight. Drive was taken out through a conventional transfer-gear arrangement to a gearbox and final drive which lived in the rear half of the massive cast-alloy lower casing – the front half being the sump.

While the engine development was in progress, the chassis engineers made ready a platform which followed established Ferrari principles, using a tubular chassis frame with the familiar oval-section main fore-and-aft tubes together with built-up assemblies of square-section tube front and rear to accept the upper suspension loads in particular. The wheelbase was very much longer than that of the V6, 100.4 ins (255 cm) compared with 92.3 ins (234 cm), in order to make room for two back seats (of a kind). The front track was opened out by more than an inch, the rear by more than two

> *angularity notable by comparison with the curves of the V6...*

inches; the suspension remained double-wishbone all round but the (then) relatively new low-profile tyres (205/70–14 instead of 215–14, Michelin XWXs being standard wear) were adopted. The brakes were minutely adjusted to cater for the rearward weight shift caused by the bigger engine and longer wheelbase, from 10.6 in discs all round to 10.5 in at the front, 10.9 in at the back, all four of them ventilated, naturally.

Through the 1960s, Pininfarina had enjoyed something close to a monopoly of Ferrari production model styling (though the actual body building was usually entrusted to the faithful Scaglietti). This all changed with the 308, for which Bertone was invited to supply the styling. He obliged with a body whose angularity was notable by comparison with the sweeping and instantly beautiful curves of the V6, and which certainly did not excite anything like the same praise. Too few people in 1974 gave Bertone credit for overcoming the considerable extra constraint of fitting in a back seat, or indeed of wanting to do his own thing and avoid any echo of Pininfarina. The Bertone body is notably compact since although (as we have seen) the wheelbase was over 8 in (20 cm) longer, the 308's overall length was only 5 in (13 cm) more than that of the 246. There was useful luggage space in the tail,

12

area and throwing in any difference in drag coefficient; in the event the extra power won out. Nobody ever claimed more than 150 mph (241 kph) for the 246GT (which was rarely subjected to genuine road test anyway) whereas the 308 clearly edged towards the mid-150s as seen in *Autocar's* 154 mph (248 kph) in well-nigh perfect conditions as it happened, in a 1976 test. That same test credited the 308GT4 with 6.9 seconds to 60 mph (97 kph) and 18.1 seconds to 100 mph (161 kph), again within a whisker of the bravest figures quoted for the V6-engined 246.

What is less clear from these figures is that the extra torque – and the different-shaped torque curve – of the V8 made the Dino GT4 a much easier car to drive if you weren't in the mood to change gear every few seconds. Again, *Autocar* makes the point that the 308 would pull not only cleanly, but strongly from 30 mph (48 kph) in its fifth gear; the lower gears were spaced for sporting driving with the 7600 rpm red line allowing 46, 64, 90 and 123 mph (74, 103, 145 and 193 kph) maxima.

As for the steering and handling, the usual comments apply with regard to the ease of getting away without power steering in a 1½ ton (1270 kg) car with very wide tyres as long as its engine and the larger part of its weight rests on the back wheels. The 308GT4's 3.3 turns of the wheel between locks sounds agreeably high-geared, until you realise that the locks in this case correspond to turning circles of well over 40 ft (12 m). The 308 is not a car to leave where you may need to wriggle out of a boxed-in parking situation. While there were few road-test complaints about the actual weight of the steering, there were plenty about kick-back on poor surfaces – an old Ferrari

though none worth talking about in the nose.

The fuel tank was 17.5 gallons (79.5 litres), 2 gallons (9 litres) more than the V6; various figures were quoted for the dry weight at the time of introduction but the concensus – supported by actual weigh-bridge figures in subsequent authoritative road tests – favours something close to 3000 lb (1360 kg) which is notably more than the 2376 lb (1080 kg) normally quoted for the late- series 246GT. What this meant, among other things, was that the increase in the V8 engine's torque output almost exactly balanced out the extra weight so that the 308GT4 2+2 (to give it its full title) ought to accelerate at least as well as the V6. Maximum speed was more a matter of trading-off the extra power against the extra frontal

failing; most of the tests said the same thing about the handling, though some were more between-the-lines than others. The 308 moved from initial understeer to power oversteer, and it was possible by lifting off in midcorner to move from the first condition to the second more quickly than was good for the average peace of mind.

Other points were more openly accepted. The back seat was there, but occupants aged more than ten or so years had a very hard time of it unless the front seat occupants were either very small, or prepared to put up with major discomfort of their own. The ride was invariably politely described as very stiff. The clutch was abominably heavy (*Autocar* measured a 50 lb load over a 5 in travel). And the cabin interior noise level, other than in gentle cruising, was extremely high.

It must have been clear to Ferrari at an early stage that parts of the motoring world would not readily forgive the killing of the Dino 246. Though it came to be grudgingly

accepted that the 308GT4 fulfilled its aims, there were plenty who wanted to see a genuine two-seater with some of the old visual appeal. In such circumstances Ferrari can move swiftly and in October 1975 one of the stars of the Paris Salon was a new Pininfarina-styled Ferrari, the 308GTB. To the casual observer, it was nearly enough (and not surprisingly, given the background) a 246GT clone although it was in truth a completely new design whose nose on closer inspection bore more than a hint of the 512B 'Boxer'. Its overall dimensions even so were startlingly close to those of the V6: half an inch wider, an inch lower and an inch wider in track.

*ABOVE The original 308 had a 3-litre carburettor-fed V8 producing 250 bhp*
*LEFT First of the 308s was Bertone's 308GT4 which appeared in 1974*
*BELOW LEFT The GT4's 2+2 interior and, BELOW, its dashboard*

## EVOLUTION

Introduced in 1974, the Bertone-styled 308 owes its model designation to 3 litres and eight cylinders. The engine is a V8 with two overhead camshafts per bank, a displacement of 2927 cc and, in its original version, four Weber carburettors. The Bertone body had an additional rear seat, hence the full designation of 308 GT4 2+2.

**1975** Pininfarina-bodied 308GTB introduced with only two seats and bearing a close resemblance to the Dino 246. The GTB's body was of glassfibre

**1977** The GTB was re-skinned in pressed steel. Open-top (Targa) 308 GTS released.

**1981** Bosch K-Jetronic fuel injection and Marelli Digiplex electronic ignition were introduced in order to meet more stringent emission regulations. New model designations were 308 GTBi and GTSi. 308 GT4 gives way to Mondial 8.

**1982** Re-designed cylinder head introduced on 308s and Mondial featuring four valves per cylinder. This system known as 'quattrovalvole'.

**1985** Capacity of the V8 engine raised from 3 to 3.2 litres.

# BUYING A USED...
# Ferrari

**Engine**
Mid-mounted, transverse V8 is super-tough and tractable

Time, perhaps, to finally do what you've long promised yourself: buy into a 328 GTB or GTS and enjoy the drive of a lifetime

STORY **RICHARD WILSHER** PHOTOGRAPHS **PETE GIBSON**

## WHY DO I WANT ONE?

**The key to your dreams?**

For many, the definitive Ferrari. Fast, lithe, sexy and just a little bit dangerous, it belongs squarely in the old school of Italian supercar design. Not quite old enough to be a classic, but not quite young enough to command silly prices, it is probably the most affordable and sensible model for the first time Ferrari buyer. Surprisingly tough and reliable, and sporting electric windows, air-con and anti-lock on late cars, it needn't be the money pit some expect.

## WHICH MODEL DO I BUY?

Prices vary widely, and UK cars are safer bets, often cheaper than those from Euro or US sources, and RHD to boot. By far the safest source, though not the cheapest, is a Ferrari dealer offering a year's Formula Warranty. If you venture outside the network you can still contact Ferrari (01784 436222) with the chassis number for any known history.

One of the virtues of the 328 is that it scarcely changed over its production run. Choose from the GTS, with its removable roof panel, or the fixed head GTB Berlinetta. The GTS Targa is generally considered the more desirable, and hence is the more expensive of the two. However, the stiffer and cheaper GTB coupé is the better to drive.

## WHAT ARE THEY LIKE TO DRIVE?

Driving a 328 is an experience to savour. Entry over the wide right-hand sill can be tricky, but no more so than it is to clamber into an Esprit. The fly-off handbrake is on the right, too, but at least that folds out of the way.

The interior is surprisingly spacious. The spindly gearstick with its five-speed gate, where first gear doglegs back to the left, screams of bygone Monza days, and it needs a firm hand as it click-clacks around the slotted gate. The clutch is heavy by today's standards, too, but that bellowing 270bhp V8 behind your head is surprisingly docile.

Just like a racer, the car feels awkward and lumpy until it warms through, when the stiff second-gear selection suddenly smoothes, the brakes respond to a touch, and the car comes alive.

Though it will dawdle at 30mph in fifth, the 328 can hit 60 in 5.5sec when urged to a screaming 7000rpm, and climb strongly to 160mph. It has huge reserves of grip and precise handling that responds best to a delicate touch; and the steering feels direct and alive in your hands.

Granny couldn't drive this car down to the shops, though. You need time to get to know it – and it's wonderfully communicative.

## ARE THEY RELIABLE?

**Cambelt changes are easy**

Ferrari technicians like this car. Simple well-proven components from fuel injection to air-con give little trouble, and the car is relatively easy to work on. The space-frame allows easy access to cambelts, so they're cheaper to change than on later monocoque cars.

They warn about low milers though – some are pristine, but some are not. It's usually down to how they're garaged. Damp seizes the suspension pins, rusts the discs, affects the trim, and starts corrosion inside the chassis and body panels despite the cars being soaked in anti-rust treatment at build.

A well used, well looked after car is generally a better bet. Any car of this age will need the occasional squirt of oil, spray of maintenance fluid or minor fiddle to remain in top shape, and a dry garage is essential. Beware any car that smells musty – that's the smell of decay. A well-maintained 328 will take you to work daily without any worries.

## WHAT SHOULD I LOOK FOR?

Any prospective purch[aser] should be taken to a Ferrari [deal]er or specialist for a thor[ough] check-over, but there are a [few] eliminators you can sort [out] for yourself.

Overall condition is im[por]tant, but check the electrics, as headlight operation an[d] the heater/air-con func[tion] mounted on the centre con[sole]. Rattles and oil drips from [the] engine speak of poor ma[inte]nance, as do squeaks [from] brakes and suspension or [any] move. Check under the nos[e for] heavy speed bump damage [and] that the silencer is not blowi[ng].

A 'Formula' sticker on [the] glass is a plus and means th[ey] should have a Ferrari 'pass[port]' so vital history can easi[ly be] checked. The chassis numb[er on] the right-hand panel next t[o the] engine will enable you to c[heck] records with Ferrari UK, wh[o are] only too happy to help. ♦

**Check cabin for loose**

### Typical prices (as advertised)

| Model | Miles | Price | Source |
|---|---|---|---|
| 85 GTS (lhd) | 38k miles | £25,000 | P |
| 86 GTS (lhd) | 52k miles | £18,000 | T |
| 87 GTB | 17k miles | £36,000 | SD |
| 87 GTS (lhd, French papers) | 56k miles | £22,000 | A |
| 87 GTS | 18k miles | £38,000 | SD |
| 88 GTS (lhd US papers) | unknown | £39,500 | A |
| 88 GTB | 34k miles | £36,000 | SD |
| 88 GTB | unknown | £35,000 | SD |
| 89 GTS | unknown | £27,000 | SD |
| 89 GTS (lhd) | 8k miles | £35,000 | SD |

SD-Ferrari Specialist Dealer, T- General Trade, P- Private, A- Internet Agency

**Chassis**
Last of the spaceframe Ferraris – easier to maintain than most

**Colour**
It has to be red

**Nose**
Check beneath for road hump scrapes

G446 YWC

**Rear brakes**
Discs can rust, cost £340 per pair, plus £134 for pads

**Exhaust**
Rear silencer a whopping £1400, can be hard to get

**Chassis number**
On right-hand chassis panel next to engine, it is the key to history check

**Door mirrors**
Priced at a sensible £120

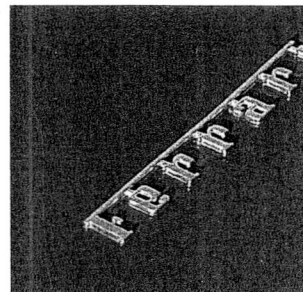

**One engine only: 3.2 V8**

G446 YWC
328 GTS

**Headlamps**
Only £35 each,
but check
pop-up action

**Suspension**
Bushes can
seize if badly
neglected

**Shock absorbers**
Fronts are
£102 each

**Brakes**
Front discs more
prone to rust
than rears. Pads
pricey at £143
a pair

**Windscreen**
A reasonable
£306

# HOW MUCH WILL IT COST ME TO RUN?

Fuel consumption of 20-35mpg is a fair expectation, while a £1203 insurance premium for a Milton Keynes-based 35-year-old on our photocar is downright cheap, assuming a Thatcham 1 alarm, £500 excess and a garage.

Whatever your mileage, you'll need the £1037/6250-mile service once a year, while the 12,500 and 25,000 services are £2440 and £3307 respectively. Cambelt change at 30,000 miles is £581.

Depreciation is currently zero, which means over 5000 miles per year, a minimum cost-per-mile of 77p is similar to an Alfa GTV 3.0's. Service is the main expense – do 10,000 miles and the cost is a modest 64p/mile. Expect around 123p/mile on 5000 miles/year when the major service is due. Tyres, costing about £600 all round, should last 10,000-15,000 miles.

**Check alloys for kerbing**

**Trad Ferrari gearshift gate needs getting used to; check air-con, electric window function and other swit**

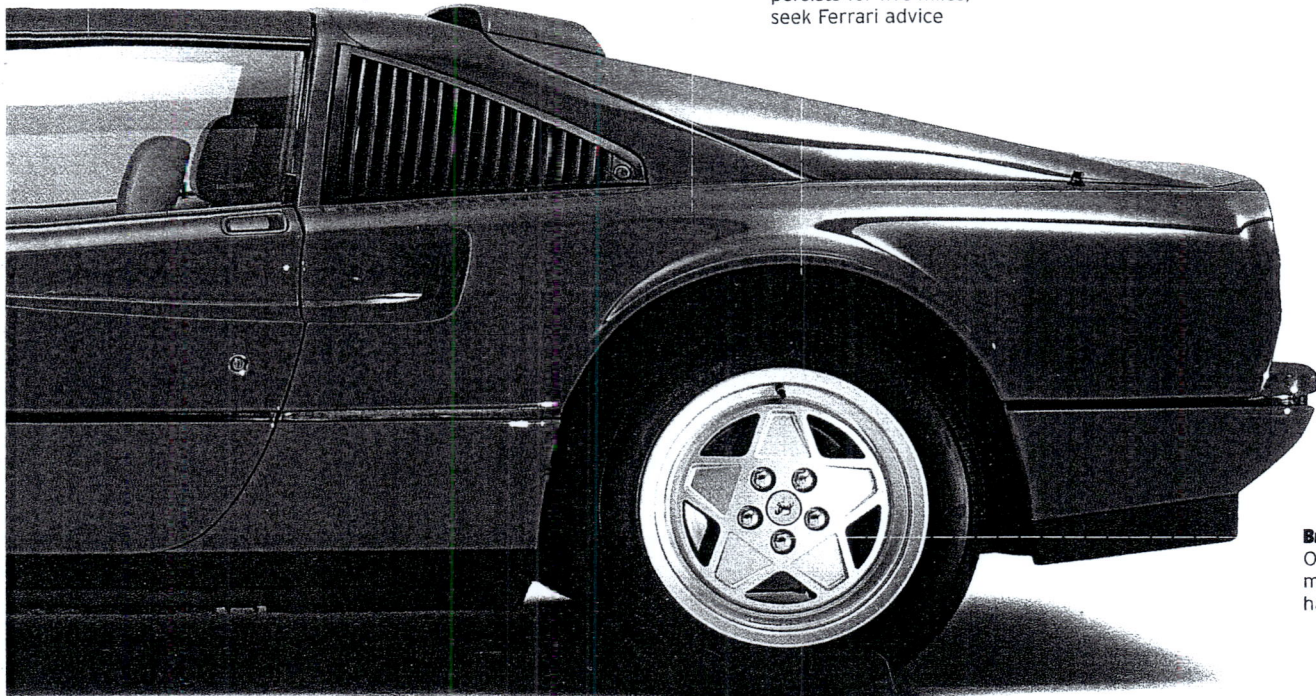

**Targa panel**
Check seals carefully for leaks – costly to replace

**Cambelt**
Change every 30k miles. Cheap for a Ferrari

**Clutch**
Heavy, and second gear balky. If problem persists for five miles, seek Ferrari advice

**Engine**
Watch for oil drips

**Brakes**
Only late model cars have anti-lock

# WHAT ELSE SHOULD I LOOK AT?

For many buyers the 328 will be competing as a status symbol with a speedboat, swimming pool or bolt-on conservatory. Which should be good news because it means there will be more 328s available for those of us who simply love cars.

The obvious alternatives are the Honda NSX, Porsche 911 and Lotus Esprit. Or, if brand new metal is important, one of the raft of blazing rally-sourced Japanese four-wheel-drive saloons, such as the Impreza Turbo or Mitsubishi Evo VII. All offer performance and handling enough to satisfy the discerning, but with one important difference: while they are always depreciating in value, the exclusive and thoroughbred 328 is not.

A 96N NSX is probably the sweetest-natured supercar for daily use; it's easy to drive and there's plenty of scope for future classic status. A 96N 3.6 911 Carrera Targa has similar virtues, but a rather more belligerent character, and by sheer weight of numbers is obviously less exclusive. And a 99T Lotus Esprit 3.5 V8 Turbo is acclaimed for its handling and classic looks, but it has an '80s feel that's not to everyone's taste. And, of course, none has the cachet of a 328.

## RIVALS

**Honda NSX**
Oft-forgotten gem that is reliable, handles superbly and runs a brilliant V6

**Porsche 911**
No car is better screwed together than the 911; if cared for, it will go forever

**Lotus Esprit Turbo**
Very dated interior, but still a head-turner and an electrifying performer

# HOW DO OWNERS RATE THEM?

Some owners love them passionately, but others don't get close to understanding the 328 psyche. A glance through the mileages of cars for sale says it all. Some have few miles and several owners – often they're treated as status symbols to be trotted out at the golf club, then ignored for months. Or perhaps they've been kept in climate-controlled garages for special occasions. Check it out before parting with your money.

Others have few owners and lots of miles. If records are complete – check with Ferrari – then these enthusiast cars are often a better bet because they've been more continuously cared for. Give the owner time to enthuse about the thing – its virtues and vices. Owning a 328 is to be custodian of a distinguished bloodline – like owning a racehorse.

## Running costs

**Ferrari 328**

**Expected servicing**
6250 mile: £1037
12,500 miles: £2440
25,000 miles: £3307
30,000 miles: £581
(cambelt)

**Fuel**
5000 miles: £800
10,000 miles: £1600

**Insurance**
**For a 35-year-old, living in Milton Keynes**
£1270 with Thatcham 2 alarm; £1203 with Thatcham 1. Excess £500.

**Depreciation**
Prices currently stable or improving.

**Cost per mile**
Depending on miles and service required and miles covered, at 5000 mile yearly use from 77-123p/mile. On 10,000 miles from around 64-110p/mile.

**THANKS TO:**
**Ferrari UK**
**01784 436222**
**www.ferrari-uk.com**
**enquiries@ferrari.co.uk**
**Primo PLC Insurance**
**01702 225400**

# VERDICT

The 328 is not a novice drive, or a car to be casually bought then taken for granted. It needs and rewards an owner who will cherish it and spend time and money on it. Race-bred in an era when men not electronics worked the controls, the 328 also calls for canny driving skills. But put the right car with the right driver and it will be a marriage made in heaven.

**AUTOCAR**
★★★★

# FERRARI 308, 328 AND MONDIAL CHASSIS NUMBERS AND REVISIONS

## (Chassis numbers for right-hand drive cars from 1974 onwards plus the details of any revisions)

| Model | Year | Chassis No. | | Remarks |
|---|---|---|---|---|
| Ferrari - 308GT4 | 1974 | 08354 | May 1974 | Basic specification. Electric windows, tinted glass and heated rear window, standard |
| | 1975 | 08918 | Jan 1975 | Electric windows, tinted glass and heated rear window, extra |
| | 1976 | 11800 | Jan 1976 | Continued |
| | | 12288 | May 1976 | Revised grille with 3 horizontal and 6 vertical strips. Ferrari motifs on bonnet, road wheels and steering wheel. Improved air-conditioning with added outlets beneath instrument panel. |
| | | 12722 | Oct 1976 | Electric windows, tinted glass and heated rear window, standard |
| | 1977 | 13120 | Jan 1977 | Continued |
| | 1978 | 13986 | Jan 1978 | Continued |
| | 1979 | 14500 | Jan 1979 | Continued |
| | 1980 | 15402 | Jan 1980 | Continued |
| | | 15474 | Dec 1980 | Discontinued. Final chassis number |
| Ferrari 308GTB | 1976 | 19149 | May 1976 | Basic specification |
| | 1977 | 20503 | Jan 1977 | Continued |
| | | 21253 | May 1977 | Last fibreglass-bodied version |
| | | 21333 | May 1977 | First steel-bodied version |
| | | 22513 | Dec 1977 | Big front spoiler optional extra. No spare wheel cover |
| | 1978 | 23207 | Jan 1978 | Continued |
| | 1979 | 26639 | Jan 1979 | Continued |

# FERRARI 328TB SERIE SPECIALE SPECIFICATION

## DIMENSION

| | | | |
|---|---|---|---|
| Wheelbase, in/mm | 96.5/2450 | Track, f/r, in/mm | 59.1/64.3/1502/1633 |
| Length, in/mm | 170.1/4320 | Width, in/mm | 74.6/1894 |
| Height, in/mm | 46.1/1170 | Ground clearance, in/mm | 4.8/122 |
| Manufacturer's base curb weight, lb | 3232 | Weight distribution, f/r % | 40/60 |
| Cargo capacity, cu ft | 7.0 | Fuel capacity, gal | 23.2 |

## ENGINE

| | |
|---|---|
| Type | V-8 liquid cooled, cast aluminium block and heads |
| Bore x stroke, in/mm | 3.35 x 2.95 / 85.0 x 75.0 |
| Displacement, ci/cc | 208/3405 |
| Compression ratio | 10.4:1 |
| Valve gear | DOHC, 4 valves/cylinder |
| Fuel/induction system | Multipoint EFI |
| Horsepower hp @ rpm, SAE net | 312 @ 7200 |
| Torque lb-ft @rpm SAE net | 229 @ 4000 |
| Horsepower/litre | 91.6 |
| Redline, rpm | 7500 |
| Recommended fuel | Unleaded premium |

## CHASSIS

### Suspension
| | |
|---|---|
| Front / Rear | Upper and lower control arms, coil springs, anti-roll bar |

### Steering
| | |
|---|---|
| Type | Rack & pinion |
| Turns, lock-to-lock | 3.0 |
| Turning circle | 39.5 |

### Brakes
| | |
|---|---|
| Front, type/dia., in | Vented discs / 11.8 |
| Rear, type/dia., in | Vented discs / 11.8 |
| Anti-lock | Standard |

### Wheels and Tyres
| | |
|---|---|
| Wheel size, in | 17 x 7.5/17 x 9.0 |
| Wheel type/material | Cast aluminium |
| Tyre size | 215/50ZR17/255/45ZR17 |
| Tyre manufacturer and model | Pirelli P-Zero |

## PERFORMANCE AND TEST DATA

| Acceleration | Sec | Acceleration | Sec |
|---|---|---|---|
| 0-30mph | 2.0 | 0.40mph | 2.8 |
| 0.50mph | 4.5 | 0.60mph | 5.6 |
| 0.70mph | 7.6 | 0-80mph | 9.2 |
| Standing quarter mile sec @ mph | | | 14.0 @ 100.0 |

| Braking | ft | Braking | ft |
|---|---|---|---|
| 30-0mph | 32 | 60-0mph | 122 |

### Handling
| | |
|---|---|
| Lateral acceleration, g | 0.96 |
| Speed through 600 ft slalom, mph | 68.8 |

# Ferrari 328 GTB/S

## Is it possible to buy a near-perfect classic Ferrari for the price of a new Alfa Romeo Brera? We think it can be done

Report by Tony Soper
Photography by Michael Ward

Ferrari prices are a fickle thing. Two years ago, a 246 Dino changed hands for around £60k, and today you need almost twice that – yet for £100k less, you can buy a similar-era 308GT4, arguably just as good a car but currently out of favour because of its wedgy shape. Surely, its time will come. So to the 308 GTB/S, a shape every bit as iconic as the 246 Dino and starting to look very undervalued, with prices ranging between £15k and £25k. But the 308 can be trouble: early ones are rather old cars now and build quality was a bit shaky as well.

Our suggestion would be the 328, a perfect first Ferrari and possibly a rather shrewd investment. With Dino prices out of reach for most, attention may well turn to the 308/328 family in the future and the 328s are undoubtedly the pick of the bunch. Most of the 308 problems were ironed out by the time the 328 appeared in 1986, and build quality was pretty good during its three-year production run.

## HISTORY

The 308's pretty Pininfarina-designed shape and Scaglietti-built body was unveiled in 1975, and was based on the earlier Bertone 308 GT4 running gear (including engine), with a traditional Ferrari steel tube chassis. The 308 GT4 dates back to 1973, and this is when the 90° V8 quad-cam engine made its debut. After 10 years of service in the 308 models, the 2926cc V8 engine was enlarged to 3185cc for the new

### TECHNICAL SPECIFICATIONS
### FERRARI 328 GTB / GTS

| | |
|---|---|
| ENGINE: | 3185cc quad-cam V8 |
| FUEL SYSTEM: | Bosch K Jetronic |
| POWER: | 270bhp @ 7800rpm |
| TORQUE: | 213lb ft @ 5500rpm |
| TRANSMISSION: | 5-speed gearbox - manual, dog-leg 1st gear |
| SUSPENSION: | Unequal-length dual wishbone, coil springs & Koni dampers |
| WHEELS & TYRES: | 7in rims, 205/55 VR16 (front); 8in rims, 225/50 VR16 (rear) |
| DIMENSIONS: | 4285mm (L), 1730mm (W) |
| KERB WEIGHT: | 1420 to 1450kg |
| TOP SPEED: | 153mph |
| 0-62MPH: | 5.6sec |

328 model (bore 83mm x stroke 73.6mm). This made the 328 the most powerful of the 308/328 family with 270bhp @ 7000rpm and the capability to actually hit that 7000rpm red line in top gear, giving a 153mph top whack. Most other 328 changes were an evolution of the 308 with subtle revisions to body lines, ABS brakes offered as an option and the front end reworked with deeper spoiler and redesigned light units. Other enhancements included the fitment of air-conditioning, electric mirrors and leather interiors.

The 328, like the previous 308, was made in two variants – GTB or GTS. GTB, meaning Gran Turismo Berlinetta, was a coupe, while the GTS (for Gran Turismo Spider) has a removable targa top section that stows behind the seats to allow open-air motoring. Both versions are mechanically identical but 328 GTBs are getting very rare now and, with just 130 original

**BARGAIN BIN?**
Italian domestic LHD 2.0 turbo, US imports, damaged or
neglected UK cars. Can be a good buy if you know what you're
looking for, but can be a money pit
**LESS THAN £22,000**
Most European LHD cars will fall into this band unless
exceptional. UK cars with mileages over 40k
**£24,000 to £26,000**
Expect near-concours condition, service history and a mileage
under 40k
**£26,000 TO £30,000**
Concours condition, full service history, bulletproof warranty
and mileage under 30k

right-hand drive cars sold in the UK, many are being
snapped up as track or competition cars. This is now
pushing up their prices.

## WHAT TO LOOK FOR

The GTS will probably be the best choice unless you
want to do serious track work, and red is by far the
most common and popular colour. Yellow, black,
'Argentinio' silver, white (very rare) and 'Chiaro' blue
metallic cars are around if you want exclusivity, but
bear in mind cars in these colours often take longer to
sell. An oddball you may encounter is the Italian
domestic 328 turbo. These were all left-hand drive and
use a 1991cc version of the V8, blown by an IHI turbo
to give 254bhp @ 6500rpm. A few may have found
their way to the UK and they tend to sell for
significantly less than their normally aspirated siblings.

Of the 7400 328s built, just 672 were supplied in
right-hand drive to the UK, resulting in a fairly small
pool of cars to choose from. Most are in good order:
you won't find basket cases to restore but there are
tired and neglected cars around, and the cost of
making them right can be significant. Expect to see
documented service history proving where the car was
originally supplied and that regular servicing has been
carried out. Top money requires low miles and there are
a suspiciously high number of low-mileage Ferraris

offered, suggesting that either they don't get out
much, or that the history warrants close inspection to
verify it. If there are gaps in the service history, or
missing MoT certificates, then be suspicious. Don't
get too picky about mileage: too little is almost as bad
as too much. Ensure evidence of regular use because
cars left idle for extended periods will probably leak oil
from every seal, if suddenly driven in anger.

Specialist or private? The established Ferrari
specialists know these models inside out, have
reputations to uphold and will often have sniffed out
the best cars for sale and offer them with warranty
back-up. Non-specialist dealers are more risky. They
may not know the ins and outs of a 328 but often still
want top money because it's shiny and red. Buying
privately is even more tricky but, approached with
caution, it can net a good deal. Specialist inspections
from the likes of www.carinspections.co.uk will provide
peace of mind and good bargaining power, and may
well be the best £300 you've ever spent. Don't hesitate

## "Don't hesitate to send a chosen specialist to inspect the car"

to send your chosen specialist to inspect the car,
whether private or trade sale, and do join the Ferrari
Owners' Club: www.ferrariownersclub.co.uk.

So, what goes seriously wrong? Well, not too much,
actually. If we were featuring the 348, there would be a
good long list but the 328 is regarded as almost
bulletproof – for a Ferrari.

## BODY

The 328 body enjoyed some zinc plating and so
corrosion is not a major problem, unlike the 308 which
does have a few rust issues. However, problems in the
vicinity of the rear wheelarch bowls are not unknown.
The bonnet is made of aluminium, the floorpan is a GRP
and steel composite, while ABS plastic is used for the

*BELOW: The 328 is an
altogether much bett[er]
than the preceding 30[8]
Although the GTS loo[ks]
nice, the trade-off is s[ome]
scuttle-shake*

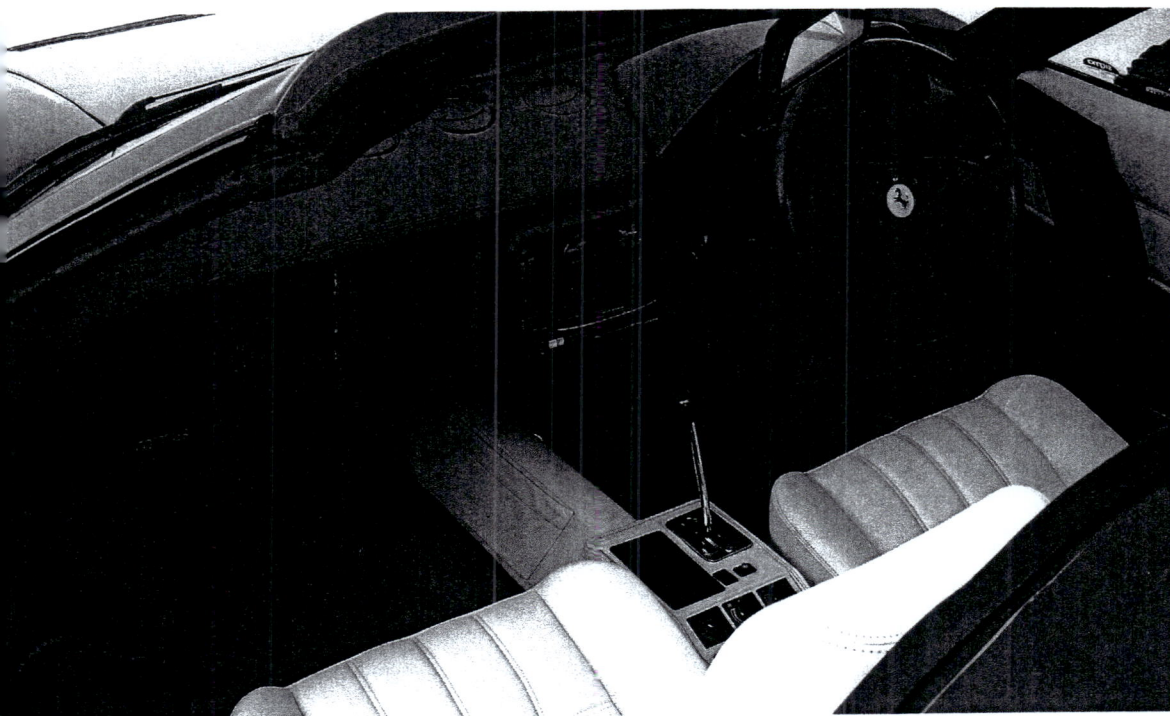

valance panels. The GTS targa top is well made but water leaks may occur in cars that have been in dehumidified storage for long periods. However, a set of replacement seals should cure the problem and these are available on the aftermarket. Do check that handbooks and toolkit are present.

## INTERIOR

Inside, expect a low seating position with a long reach to a non-adjustable Momo steering wheel with colourful, orange, back-lit Veglia instrumentation. In fact, it is possible to adjust the rake of that Momo wheel to make yourself a little bit more comfortable, but there is no visible adjustment lever. Instead, you must lie on your back in the footwell, remove the cover beneath the steering cowl and expose two retaining bolts, which can be loosened to allow the angle to be reset. If the car you are looking at has an in-car entertainment system fitted, then it will be aftermarket, since the cars were supplied new without any factory-fit option. Expect a well-presented interior, seats, door cards and console. Leather wears well but retrimming is expensive, so budget accordingly.

## ELECTRICS

The electrics give very little trouble, although the switchgear (like the mirror switches) can sometimes play up due to inactivity. Often these components are drawn from other manufacturers' parts bins; for instance the mirror switches are also found on various Lancia and BMW models and the indicator stalks have a Fiat Ducato look about them! Electric windows can be slow. Dismantling, cleaning and lubricating all the moving parts often alleviates the problem and, if not, a permanent solution can be obtained from www.ferrariwindow.com. The engine management control is by Marelli Microplex for ignition and old-school Bosch K Jetronic for fuel. This is a simple and reliable arrangement that asks only for periodic cleaning by way of maintenance. However, the Microplex system is long out of production and, if it does go down, it will need specialist attention. Most ignition problems can be traced to the coil packs, which are readily replaced.

Air-conditioning was an option from new and, if the system is weak, check the refrigerant type. It would originally have been R12, which is now banned, and very difficult to have serviced these days, but most will have been converted to R134a, which means a simple vacuum and re-gas should be possible.

## ENGINE

The engine is very well proven, the main requirements being regular oil and filter changes (Agip Sint 10w40 or

*ABOVE: Red with Crema hide are classic Ferrari colours. Some say that conservative blue or silver cars could be better looked after than red*

## PRODUCTION HISTORY

**FERRARI 328GTB - 1985**
Total factory
production: 1344
UK RHD: 130 cars (53 had
ABS brakes)
UK launch price: £32,200

**FERRARI 328GTS - 1985**
Total factory
production: 6068
UK RHD: 542 cars (292 had
ABS brakes)
UK launch price: £32,250

**SAMPLE SERVICE COSTS**
(including parts, plus VAT)
6000-mile service: £380
18,000-mile service: £700
Timing belts: £360
Clutch: £800

**328 GTS**

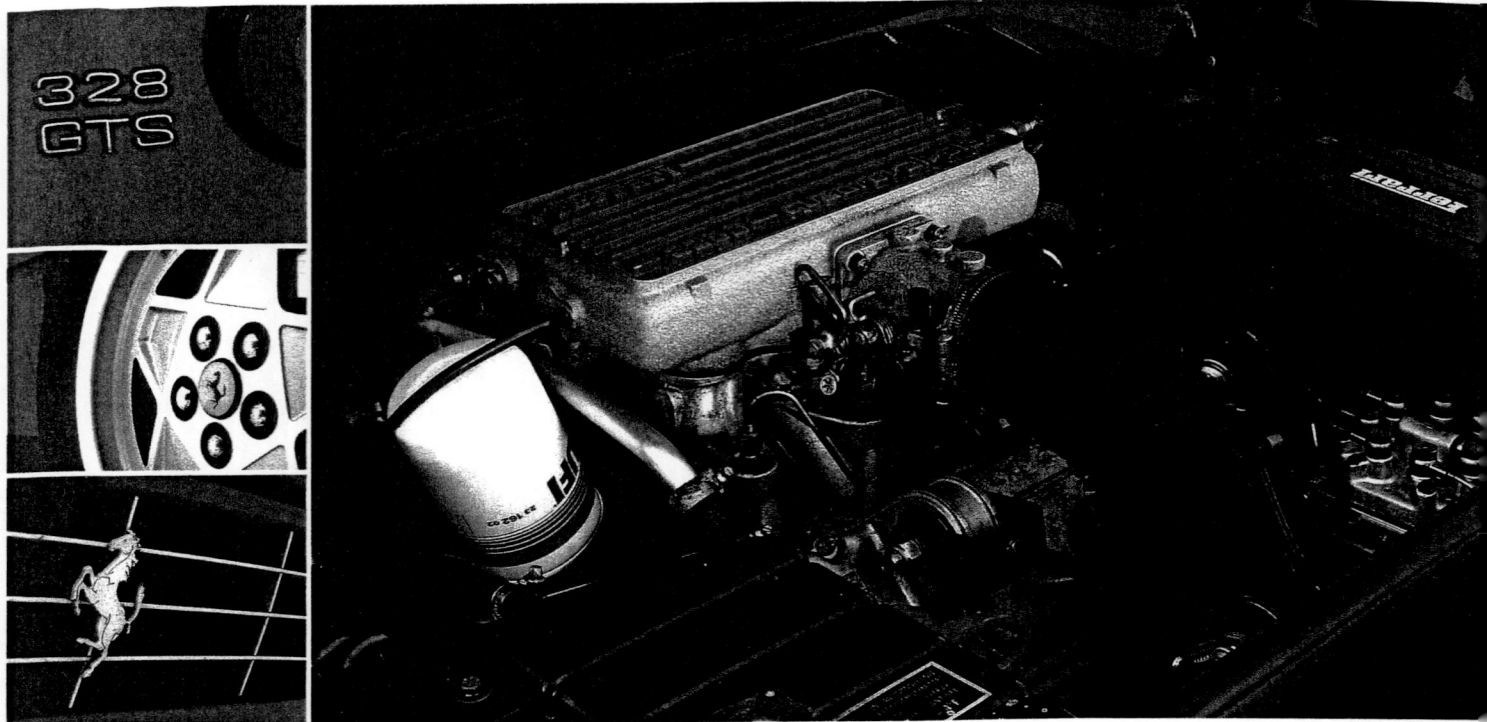

other premium brand) and a check that the timing belts are in date. Actual breakage of the belt is very rare, and then only on neglected cars, but Ferrari says you should replace them every two years and, given the cost of the engine parts, you would be wise to comply. Breakage will bend exhaust valves at best, considerably more at worst. Expect to pay a specialist between £400 and £500 to supply and fit new belts. Tensioners are usually checked at two years and replaced every four. Be aware that the engine has aluminum/Nikasil liners so use of a quality oil is vital as damage to the Nikasil coating means new liners: a very expensive job.

## HOME SERVICING

If you fancy having a bash at the belts yourself, it can be done without disturbing the engine. Access is via the rear wheel houses. Remove the RHR wheel, brake disc, inner cover and fuel tank (not essential, but gives more room). Disconnect the air-conditioning compressor if fitted and hang to one side, loosen the alternator and pivot out of the way, take off the timing-belt covers. Now, turn the crank to give cylinder number 1 at top dead centre and align the cam-pulley indicators. Mark all pulley positions with paint, loosen the three bolts securing the tensioners and remove, and the belts can now be eased off. As the man from Haynes always says, refitting is the reverse of dismantling: ease the new belts over the unflanged cam pulley last and then check the cam pulleys align with your marks because they will probably have moved due to valve spring tension. When refitted and tensioned, rotate the engine several times by hand, and check, double check and check again that all your marks line up before firing up. It may be a Ferrari, but it's fitted with a conventional engine and if you can change the timing belt on an Alfa V6, then you can do it on a 328 as well.

*ABOVE: Providing the engine is warmed up thoroughly before use, it is pretty much bulletproof. Even with a capacity of 3.2 litres it still has to be worked quite hard to get the best out of it*

*RIGHT: The 328 is quite a compact car by modern standards. Driving visibility is very good and the car is easy to handle in today's traffic conditions*

## TRANSMISSION

The gearbox rarely gives real grief, bar some notchiness around first and second gear when the oil is cold, but the shift is often awkward at low speeds. The shiny lever gate looks great but makes city driving a chore; however, at speed you can expect slick shifts. The clutch is very strong but, if it does need to be replaced, budget up to £1000 for a specialist to sort it out.

## BRAKES AND SUSPENSION

Brakes and suspension are reliable but check the hubs for bearing play. Variants with ABS can be spotted by a greater wheel offset to house bulkier calipers and the ATE-sourced system is very reliable. Ride quality should be firm and precise, without excessive harshness or bodyroll.

## EXHAUST SYSTEM

Exhausts and mountings can corrode and seize, but systems are readily available from the aftermarket and a complete stainless steel replacement will cost around £750, supplied and fitted. European cars did not have catalytic converters but US cars did. Cooling systems are critical. Coolant header tanks sometimes leak due to corrosion and, if the pressure cap is original, it will be almost 20 years old now and certainly due for replacement.

## WHEELS AND TYRES

Original equipment fare will be 16in five-spoke 'star' pattern alloys, in silver, with Goodyear NCT or Pirelli P7 rubber. Aftermarket wheels rarely look as good as the stock items and can make the car more difficult to sell, so, if alternatives are fitted, expect the originals to come with the car or make a price adjustment.

## SERVICING

Parts supply is very good for the 328. There's not much that can't be sourced, thanks to the likes of Eurospares (www.usedferraris.net) or Maranello Concessionaires (www.ferraripart.co.uk) in the UK. Also worth a look is the US-based Ferrari parts exchange to take advantage of the weak dollar (www.ferraripartsexchange.com), while Norwood Performance in Texas offers tempting dollar-priced upgrades for engine and brake systems (www.norwoodperformance.com).

Here in the UK, there's a network of specialists with huge experience of maintaining these cars, and the likes of Foskers at Brands Hatch offer competitive service deals. Tel 01474 874555; www.foskers.com. ▮▮

## THANKS

Thanks to Foskers at Brands Hatch, where the featured low-mileage, concours-quality example is currently offered for sale at a most favourable price. Tel 01474 874555 www.foskers.com

## OUR CHOICE

There really is little reason to fear taking the plunge and joining the Ferrari family. Our pick would be a red 328GTB or GTS with the Crema interior and preferably under 40,000 miles, with that all-important service history. At the time of writing, the Autotrader website has 15 cars for sale. At the bottom of the price range is a left-hand drive, imported GTS turbo with a £22k asking price, while at the top of the market, respected specialist Nick Cartwright is offering a 23,000-miler GTS in concours condition for £32k. Such a car will always be an investment, probably appreciating a couple of thousand pounds a year, giving virtually cost-free Ferrari ownership.

A Ferrari is on most people's list when a big Pools win is under discussion. The stuff of which such reputations are made is a combination of high performance, superb roadholding, a cossetting interior, and the best of good looks. On each of these counts, the Ferrari Dino 308GTB scores most of the points that are there to be won.

Of course, there are shortcomings. The price, for a start, is enough to ensure that the Pools win must be a big one. There are others. Like the mistaken choice of facia covering that allows bad reflections in the windscreen, and the fact that the beautiful lines spell out "design triumphs over engineering" to the extent that there is no room for a proper spare wheel.

But when the open road beckons, when a touch of adrenalin is wanted and the spirits need to soar, this particular Ferrari is the best tonic available. There is no mistaking the admiring looks of passers-by of any age and the questioning yet furtive look inside to ascertain "who is the lucky so-and-so who owns that?"

Enthusiast's anticipation began rising when it became known that Ferrari's successor to the much-loved Dino 246GT was being designed by the same sure hands at Pininfarina. Many had not liked the hard-edged looks of the interim Bertone-designed 308GT4 two plus two. Not surprisingly, when the long, low dart-shaped 308GTB was revealed at Paris in 1975, it was swamped with admirers.

The 308GTB, built by Scaglietti, is the first production Ferrari with a glass-fibre body. Its finish is superb. Very much a two-seater, it has little room even for discarded coats in the cockpit, and requires a wide central tunnel to take water cooling pipework to the front of the car and the gearchange and handbrake linkages to the back. The height, at only 3ft 10in, could pose problems but the reclined seating position, wide door opening and minor intrusion of the roof into the door opening combine to make entry, exit, and the seating position comfortable.

Suspension parallels that of the GT4 two plus two with double wishbones and coil springs front and rear as well as substantial anti-roll bars at both ends. The low body don't permit very much suspension travel, and the need to control roll is important.

The familiar three-litre V8 dohc engine is mounted traversely in the middle of the car and the drive is taken from the left end of the engine via the clutch to a set of drop gears that reverse the direction of drive from right-to-left back to left-to-right towards the five-speed, all-synchromesh gearbox. The gears sit in their own separate sump partitioned off from the engine sump.

Both the 308GT4 two plus two and 308GTB Dino engines produce the same power output of 255bhp at 7700rpm. The GTB's sump, however, is dry, taking the oil capacity up from 16 to 19.5 pints, aiding cooling, reducing engine height and avoiding oil surge. As well as the high power of the V8, its strong 210lb ft of torque at 5000rpm in a car weighing only 2870lb means that you're not always changing gear to sustain rapid progress.

The 308GTB's shape demands that it can only be a two-seater, but the long tail does permit reasonable luggage accommodation.

**Slipped in sideways just behind the seats, the three-litre V8 is a torquey, free-revving gem**

To get at the boot, one must first raise the engine cover and, with this out of the way, a neat, zipped, pvc cover opens to reveal a deep, full width, carpeted area in which the jack, wheelbrace and toolkit also live. There is additional minimal luggage space beneath the front bonnet.

Favourable weight distribution, good aerodynamic shape, excellent gearing and the unusually high power-to-weight ratio give the Ferrari exceptional performance. The speeds it attains are deceptively fast since there is little wind and road noise.

Wide tyres, the limited slip differential and inherently good traction ensure that the step-off from rest (even when searching for ultimates) is without drama. After a little wheelspin, the GTB rockets forward towards the 7700rpm maximum engine speed. First gear is out to the left and back

**Ducts feed air to engine; fuel filler is hidden behind black grate. Gfrp body's finish is superb**

**Even among Ferraris, 308 is one of Pininfarina's loveliest designs. Its details ooze sensuality**

in the gated gearchange, but there is enough strong spring centering to ensure that the change to second gear can be very fast. The improved synchromesh cannot be beaten, and the only considerations that can slow the change are the need for full clutch clearance for each change and the inertia of the long linkage. Second gear takes you to 65mph with the magic 60mph coming up in 6.5sec when it's time to whip the gearlever back into third to rush the car onwards to 92mph. You get to 80mph in the fine time of 10.8sec. The change to fourth gear is again a dog-leg forward and out to the right, and you must take care to push deliberately against the spring pressure.

The time to 100mph is a quick 17.0sec with the quarter-mile despatched in 14.8sec at 93mph. Fourth gear is good for 124mph with 120mph passing in just 25.0 sec —

**Cabin is very habitable: comfortable seats, good vision, ambiance. But facia reflects in screen**

perhaps half the time it has taken you to read this paragraph.

Acceleration in each gear reveals the useful spread of torque, as well as the absence of snatch in the driveline or holes in the torque curve. One can accelerate from as low as 10mph in third and there is no feeling that fifth gear is an overdrive: it will pull away strongly from 30mph.

To check the top speed we needed a long run in before the car settled at 7050rpm (7150rpm on the test car's slightly optimistic tachometer), equivalent to 154mph This is 4mph less than Ferrari's claim but we had overnight luggage and test gear aboard which, in a car with a rear boot, can be enough to bring the nose up and to knock off the last few mph. We were grateful for still air during our timed runs; the slightest cross wind leads to very disconcerting weaving above 130 mph.

Our overall fuel figure of 19.2mpg is good for the class, stemming from a higher than average amount of open road driving. Even so, careful owners should better 20mpg regularly.

The aesthetically satisfying lines of the 308 cannot promise very much wheel travel, and the suspension settings for both springs and dampers are necessarily hard. At low speeds on less than smooth surfaces, the 308GTB's ride is very bumpy, with potholes giving rise to much crashing and banging. However, once into the mid-range of the car's performance the ride improves greatly, and only the worst of undulations are not soaked up adequately. At very high speed the ride gives great confidence, with no tendency to pitch, and not a trace of float. Under most conditions the handling is reassuring too, although there is a strong tendency to follow camber changes, especially at the front, and a strong grip on the wheel should be avoided.

There is some kickback through the steering. Ferrari argues that some is necessary for the right level of feel, and the steering does give all the right messages. Since the predominant characteristic is extra understeer with extra speed, the feeling of increased weight in the steering is very pleasantly pro rata. Though 3.3 turns lock-to-lock might suggest high-geared steering, the turning circle is a dreadful 40ft. The gearing could be higher without parking becoming too heavy. On the move, where the slightly low gearing helps avoid any suddenness in steering reaction, the ratio is about right.

While the handling is generally praiseworthy, you need to careful about the way the 308GTB responds sudden throttle closure. While the natural tendency is understeer, if the accelerator is released in mid-corner the weight transfer means an immediate tightening of your line. This is, of course, usually no penalty and can be used to advantage but demands caution on wet or slippery roads. Once you've killed understeer by lifting off the accelerator, immediate power application can set up a satisfying four-wheel drift which will please skilled drivers immensely.

However, the relatively short wheelbase and low polar moment of inertia mean that extreme angles of drift cannot be held despite the quickness and accuracy of the steering. The 70-aspect Michelin XWX radial ply tyres give excellent roadholding and splendid traction on wet surfaces but are guilty of mild bump-thumping which the suspension compliance does not completely isolate. The brakes are large and thick ventilated discs with twin circuits, a single in-line servo and a rear pressure-limiting valve. A feeling of being

Retractable headlights keep nose smooth

over-servoed at low speeds is only to ensure bite from the hard linings and well-cooled discs. At speed the system gives reassuring performance through close progression in efficiency with increased pedal effort, coupled to total alck of fade.

Happily, in line with its inherent refinement, the noises the GTB makes are all pleasant. The exhaust is subdued at most speeds and only full throttle in confined surroundings could annoy anyone. There is a slight increase in wind noise at speed.

The Ferrari is well-equipped. Electric windows, tinted glass, a laminated windscreen with tinted top section, heated rear window and leather upholstery are all standard. The options list is confined to air-conditioning, metallic body paint, and wide wheels (with tyres of the same size).

Once in the seats the occupants are comfortably positioned, with generous rearward and backrest rake adjustment. There is a full complement of clear, round instruments: speedo and rev counter,with smaller dials for oil pressure, fuel level and water temperature set between them. Low down to the right of the facia are an oil temperature gauge and a clock.

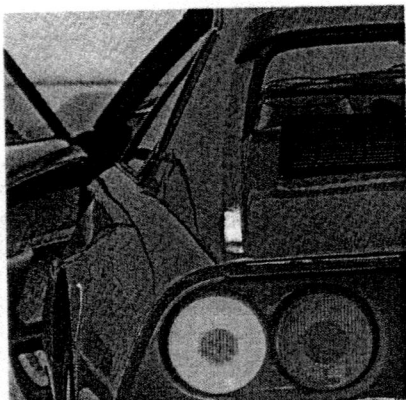
Traditional round rear lights blend with lines

Major function controls are operated by three fingertip stalks, with wash/wipe to the right of the steering wheel and indicators and lights to the left. The heating, ventilation and air-conditioning controls are on a panel between the seats.

The big foot pedals allow heel-and-toe action. The driving position is typically Italian with the steering wheel set flat, forcing a knees-up/arms stretched pose.

The 308GTB has only two serious drawbacks: the clutch pedal effort which, at 60lb is heavyweight, and made more wearing because the full 7in of travel is needed to engage the gears smoothly and quickly; and the facia top covering. In strong overhead lighting at night or when you're heading towards the sun, the reflections in the windscreen are bad enough to be hazardous.

All other aspects of comfort are strong, like seats that do not cause aches, good visibility (except at angled junctions), and a wealth of on-board stowage space. How-ever, the wipers are not fast enough and the (splendid) pop-up headlamps cannot be used for daylight flashing.

Despite its lengthy run, the accelerator linkage is excellent, giving smooth progressive response that helps to avoid jerkiness. Access to the V8 is not good. To change the plugs of the front bank of cylinders would take all day, and there seems to be twice as much of everything as there needs to be. Two coils, two timing belt tensioners, two fuel filters and two contact breakers. In fact, with the help of the excellent handbook, it would be possible for all relevant service items to be handled by an enthusiastic owner.

If you didn't know the body was glass-fibre you'd never guess. There is no smell of glass-fibre, the doors shut with a delightful dull thud, and the paint finish is as good as steel. A major advantage will be rust resistance, further guaranteeing the 308GTB's place in treasured collections in the years ahead. This is so good in most respects that the short-comings stand out like sore thumbs. The clutch pedal effort is unjustifiably high and out of character. The large turning circle and length of the 308GTB do not allow for easy parking. The loss of high-speed stability in cross-winds is regrettable and hard to understand.

But, all round, we're lost in admiration for the superb mechanical engineering, the standard of finish, the performance, the beauty and the all-round efficiency. The 308GTB is outrageously appealing. ●

## FACTFILE

### ENGINE
Layout 90deg V8, 2926cc, dohc
Bore/stroke 81x71mm
Max power 255bhp at 7700rpm
Max torque 210lb ft at 5000rpm
Installation Mid, transverse, rear-drive

### TRANSMISSION

| Gear | ratio | mph/1000 |
|---|---|---|
| Fifth | 0.918 | 21.8 |
| Fourth | 1.244 | 16.1 |
| Third | 1.693 | 12.0 |
| Second | 2.353 | 8.4 |
| First | 3.418 | 5.8 |
| Final drive | 3.71 | |

### DIMENSIONS
Length 4229mm Width 1719 Height 1120
Wheelbase 2390 Kerb weight 1300kg

### SUSPENSION
Front Unequal A-arms, coils, telescopic dampers, anti-roll bar
Rear Unequal A-arms, coils, telescopic dampers, anti-roll bar
Steering Rack and pinion, unassisted
Wheels and tyres 6.5x14in; 205/70VR14 Michelin
Brakes Ventilated discs 10.8in (f) 11in (r) servoed

### PERFORMANCE
MAXIMUM SPEEDS

| Gear | mph | rpm |
|---|---|---|
| Fifth (mean) | 154 | 7050 |
| (best) | 154 | 7050 |
| Fourth | 124 | 7700 |
| Third | 92 | 7700 |
| Second | 65 | 7700 |
| First | 44 | 7700 |

ACCELERATION FROM REST

| True mph | Time (secs) | Speedo |
|---|---|---|
| 30 | 2.3 | 28 |
| 40 | 3.3 | 40 |
| 50 | 5.1 | 50 |
| 60 | 6.5 | 61 |
| 70 | 8.7 | 71 |
| 80 | 10.8 | 81 |
| 90 | 13.8 | 91 |
| 100 | 17.0 | 102 |
| 110 | 20.4 | 112 |
| 120 | 25 | 124 |

Standing quarter mile 14.8sec at 93mph
Standing kilometre 26.9sec at 124mph

ACCELERATION IN GEARS

| mph | 5th | 4th | 3rd | 2nd |
|---|---|---|---|---|
| 10-30 | - | - | 5.1 | 3.3 |
| 20-40 | - | 6.4 | 4.1 | 2.7 |
| 30-50 | 9.5 | 5.5 | 3.5 | 2.6 |
| 40-60 | 8.4 | 5.0 | 3.6 | 4.8 |
| 50-70 | 7.8 | 5.1 | 3.6 | - |
| 60-80 | 7.2 | 5.1 | 3.9 | - |
| 70-90 | 7.7 | 5.5 | 4.4 | - |
| 80-100 | 8.8 | 6.0 | - | - |
| 90-110 | 9.2 | 6.7 | - | - |
| 100-120 | 10.2 | 8.0 | - | - |

Average mpg 19.2

Test date 3 October 1976

# Owning a 308GTB

Cropley's '76 plastic-bodied 308GTB provided reliability as well as huge motoring pleasure. Practicality wasn't bad either. Now wishes he'd kept it...

When I paid £12,000 in 1984 for a red Ferrari 308GTB I thought I'd paid too much. The right price seemed around £10,000, but after looking at some bubbly metal-bodied versions I plumped for an early (1976) version with glass-fibre body. The plastic 308 was made for only a year, then Ferrari changed to steel: the gfrp bodies were costly and, anyway, buyers expected expensive cars to be metal.

Truth be to d, I'd been looking for a £10,000 Porsche 911 until two things happened. First, I discovered that all affordable Porsches had done lots of miles. Second, a friend turned to me one day and muttered: "The person who has the chance to own a Ferrari and doesn't take it needs shooting.' After two years and 12,000 miles was it clear how just how right he had been. By then my 308GTB had traversed some brilliant roads, and filled me with the pure joy of driving. It had also

proved what the experts said: that major Ferrari components were tough. My only problems were a duff rear wheel bearing and a weep from a heater pipe.

Still, I lost my nerve and decided to sell. The Ferrari boom had begun and the car left me with £19,000 in the hand. The next bloke drew £25,000, the one after him took £40,000. The car's still with its third owner since me, and I know he loves it because we still talk. That's how it should be. ●

**Steve Cropley**

# FERRARI DINO 308

Whatever the car, and no matter how exotic it is, examples will eventually find their way into the secondhand car market. Even though some of the Italian "supercars" are terrifically fast, very expensive and - by definition - rare, there seem to be substantial numbers of them in this country, and to the lucky buyer with the money and inclination a surprising number are now on the secondhand lists. Such a car is the Ferrari 308 family, which has now been on sale here since 1974. It forms the ideal basis for a Buying Secondhand survey of this type of car; it is a model, which is very competently served by the Ferrari dealerships in Great Britain. Unlike some other "supercar" marques which (theoretically) compete with it, a Ferrari is not a car which you buy in hope, and sell after bitter experience. It will never be a cheap car to maintain, but you *will* be able to maintain it.

Even though Ferrari are dominant in this sector of the business, the marque does have rivals, even though some of them have now fallen by the wayside. As the most recent "small Ferrari", it had to fight for its sales against the mid-engined Lamborghini Urraco and the mid-engined Maserati Merak. The most important rival, however, is the Porsche 911 range, which sells much more strongly in most markets in the world. On price grounds, even though they are front-engined and have much larger engines, we consider than the Jaguar XJS and the Mercedes-Benz 350/450SL/SLC cars attract the same type of customers.

### Defining the Pedigree

There are two rather different types of "Ferrari 308". One, the Ferrari 308GTB/GTS type, is the pure mid-engined two-seater, and the true successor to the much loved Dino 246GT/GTS cars of 1969-73. The other is the occasional four-seater car carrying the unwieldy title of 308GT4 2 + 2, originally badged as a Dino, but now known as a pure Ferrari.

Both cars, however, share the same common multi-tubular chassis layout (a design feature which has persisted on Ferraris for many years), though the two cars wheelbases are different. That of the 308GTB is exactly the same as that of the 246GT, at 7ft 8in, while that of the more spacious 308GT4 2 + 2 is 8ft 4.4in. The difference is just enough to account for the tiny "+2" seating of the bigger car.

Both cars have the same transversely positioned four-cam V8 engines, mounted immediately behind the passenger compartment and ahead of the rear wheels independent coil spring suspension, and both have four-wheel disc brakes.

### Engines and Transmission

Mechanically indeed, they are virtually identical, though the three types of body shell each have their own special features. In each case, too, although they are relatively "little Ferraris", they are tremendously fast, and expensive to run, so the potential insurance problems and the driving skills required can well be imagined. Not even the GT4 2+2 could be considered, in any way, as a family man's car.

All the 308 models share the same engine/transmission package. The engine is a 90 degree twin-cam V8 of 2,926cc, and the fact that its bore and stroke is the same as that of the 4.4 litre V12 Ferraris is no more than a production convenience, for there is really virtually nothing in common between the V8 and any other previous Ferrari engine. The power output is a massive 255bhp (DIN) at 7,700rpm, and peak torque of 209lb ft. is developed at the relatively high speed of 5,000rpm. In unit with this expensive, almost hand-made, engine is a five speed all-synchoromesh gearbox, all indirect, and the final drive is also tucked behind and close to the main engine/gearbox power pack. At 1,000rpm in top gear (at which no self-respecting Ferrari owner would ever labour his engine) the cars are doing just 21.8mph.

The only real difference between the two engines is that the GT4 2+2 has a normal wet sump, while the 308GTB and GTS two-seater models have dry sump installations. In more than six years of production there appear to have been few significant changes to this unit.

A limited-slip differential is a feature of this transmission, and our testers found that the engine was not only powerful (as you would expect), but that it was also remarkably docile.

Although neither version is available in Britain, it is worth noting that a 208GT 4 2+2 is sold in Europe as an "oil crisis" special, with a reduced-bore 1.991cc engine and a mere 170bhp, and that for sale in North America the magnificent engine has to be throttled down to 240byp.

## Body Choice and Model Range

There are three different models on the same basic mechanical layout, two on the short wheelbase, and having two seats with virtually no space even for stowage behind them, and one on a lengthened wheelbase with 2 + 2 seating.

The 308GT4 2 + 2 was the first of these cars to become available (from May 1974 in Britain) with a coachbuilt steel body by Bertone. Our testers think that the rear seats are certainly only large enough for willing and athletic children, and are quite impractical for adults to occupy for a long journey. There is a rear stowage box, which is above and behind the line of the rear axle. The car has a somewhat stubby style, and since the two cars were both shaped by Bertone it is not surprising that there is a superficial resemblance to the Lamborghini Uracco as well. Even for a car of this price there are expensive extras which many owners might have considered essential; from the beginning of 1975, the previously standard items, namely electric windows, tinted glass and a heated rear window all became optional. When we tested the car in 1976 the price of these options was nearly £200.

The GT4 2 + 2, incidentally, was originally called a Dino, rather than a true Ferrari, but it was finally officially christened a "Ferrari" from mid-1976.

There was never any doubt about the two-seaters, both styled by Pininfarina but constructed for Ferrari by Scaglietti. These, paradoxically enough, were never given the "Dino" title, even though they used the old Dino 246's chassis, and were more-or-less direct replacements. The two-seater 308GTB, which was a fixed head coupé, or Berlinetta, originally had a steel hull, but glass-fibre skin panels (this was an innovation for Ferrari), but by the beginning of 1977 steel-skinned versions were being exported to the United States and from May 1977 all 308GTB's were constructed with conventional steel-skinned body shells. The 308GTS, which has only been on sale in Britain since the beginning of 1978, is very rare here, and is like the 308GTB, except that it has a detachable roof panel, which converts it into a Spyder; all 308GTS's have steel body shells.

Like the GT4 2+2, the GTB/GTS cars have no stowage space up front, and a reasonably spacious "boot" in the extreme tail. It is probably not at all significant that no maximum payload is quoted by the factory for the two-seater cars, as there is no way that they can carry more than two people and their luggage.

All three cars have hidden headlamps, which fold upwards for use. Their bodies are hand finished and fragile. Apart from the general level of costs, it must be inducement to stay well clear of traffic nudges in a 308GTB, for you cannot merely replace a front wing; the entire nose section must be changed.

## Testers' Opinions

Even though they have the same basic chassis, there is quite a lot of difference between the behaviour of the two types. The 308GTB.GTS cars are ultimately more sporting, and more responsive, with direct steering, and the ability to be driven really fast on twisting roads. The GT4 2+2 is rather larger and a little heavier, and feels it; our testes noted considerably more understeer in normal conditions. Both cars have restricted wheel movement and suffer from a hard ride. A Ferrari road car, even for that money, makes few concessions to comfort at the expense of road holding. Exhaust and general mechanical noise, however, was rather less than might have been feared; driven at normal speeds the Ferrari should not attract too much attention from do-gooders and spoil-sports.

## Performance and Economy

It is indeed interesting to have to report on a range of cars which *all* have tremendous performance. Our testers found that both styles of 308 could achieve 154mph when flat out (and there is nowhere that you can achieve this legally in Britain, and precious few places where you could take your licence in your hands and see if we were right!), that both would accelerate to 100mph in about 18 seconds, and that they could both regularly notch up fuel economy of better than 20mpg. The two-seater cars, naturally, are a little faster if you insist, but very few other cars on the road could outsprint *any* of the 308 family, and probably none in greater security. All this, mark you, can be achieved with greater running economy than in - say - a 3 litre Porsche 9111, a Jaguar XJ-S or a Mercedes Benz 350SLC. On this occasion, therefore, we do not have to balance performance against economy and against accommodation. If you can afford one, choose the Ferrari 308, which suits your space requirements and your personality.

## Model Availability and Choice

Because of the character of these ultra-fast cars, and their original range of prices, the market is strictly limited, but then so is the demand for secondhand examples. There is a goodly sprinkling of 308GT4 2 + 2's and 308GTB's in the trade, however, and you could certainly become a Ferrari 308 owner for comfortably less than £6,000 if you were not too particular about condition and mileage. Don't, incidentally, expect the rising price of petrol to have much effect on prices, as fuel costs are only a tiny proportion of running costs where a Ferrari is concerned, and condition and service history is a much more important factor.

If your fancy turns to a 308GTS you will have great difficulty in finding one at any price, so you will have to pay at least £14,000 for the privilege. Expect to find most of the optional extras fitted to most cars, though this doesn't affect the asking price too much.

To find the secondhand stock of Ferraris, you should make for the 16 Ferrari dealers in the United Kingdom (one only in Scotland, one only in Northern Ireland and none at all in Wales by the way), or to the few experienced independent traders like Modena Engineering of East Horsley. There are several official Ferrari dealers in London and the Home Counties, and a trio in the Midlands; in the countryside you will have to travel a long way.

## Service and Spare Parts

In both instances this is an important part of Ferrari 308 ownership. The Ferrari importation and servicing chain is administered by Maranello Concessionaires Ltd., from headquarters in Egham, Surrey, who have held the concession for many successful years. In the whole of the UK, however, there are only 16 Ferrari specialist dealerships, including one each in London, Birmingham, Leicester, near Coventry, Manchester, Glasgow and Belfast. Even if you can afford to buy a secondhand Ferrari (lucky you - congratulations), you should consider the inconvenience *and* the cost of sending your car many miles to a garage competent enough to provide service and repairs. Never, never, trust it to a garage which does not understand Ferraris.

Spare a though, too, for the cost of service, which should be frequent (every 3,000 miles), painstaking and - unavoidably - costly. The price of most spare parts is horrifying by any standards. Purely as an example, we can quote the price of a single Michelin XWX tyre as £101.50.

## WHAT TO LOOK FOR

### Body

Here is the good news - a Ferrari is a joy to look at, and a pleasure to own. The bad news is that in general the quality of the steel bodywork is probably less than the most ordinary of mass production saloons. Even on two year old or three year old cars, therefore, look out for rust. It is not a structural problem (the car has a self-supporting tubular chassis frame), but it can be very disfiguring, and costly to repair. For this reason alone, it makes the glass-fibre bodied (1975 to early 1977) 308GTBs even more desirable. Visually there is no change, except that you can identify a glass fibre 308GTB by the mould break near the top corners of the screen.

On steel bodied cars, look for rust inside the wheel arches, behind the front wheel arch on the outside of the bodywork, along the sills, and under the tail near the splash area.

Many 308GTBs are strictly "toys" and will have received use only in fine weather, and probably "one-up" carpet interior trimming is not of the highest standard, and entry' exit is not at all easy, so check for general condition of trim and kick panels. Look very carefully at the windscreen for evidence of stone chipping, as the car is very low, as is the nose, and this sort of damage seems to occur more often (and screens are expensive....)

As so often happens with exotic Italian cars, there can sometimes be infuriating electrical problems. Insist, therefore, or a full systems check of all electrical systems, while static and while the car is in motion. Do not, however, confuse wet or cold weather behaviour with faulty electrics, as the car is temperamental enough even when working properly! Likely trouble spots with an older and neglected car would be the headlamp operation, or the electric window lifts.

The bodywork, though simple, is delicately formed, so be extra careful in your inspection, for slipshod accident repairs, particularly around the vulnerable nose and tail areas.

Air conditioning, though not standard, is fitted to many cars, and we feel that it is extremely desirable, even in the British climate. Red, incidentally is *the* most sought after colour.

### Mechanical

The *caveat* here is to look for a car with a service history which can be authenticated. A 308 without a history is usually one which has been neglected. You have been warned. Service is required every 3,000 miles which many owners omit to have done. It is sad but true that many Ferrari owners think they can get away without meticulous service - and it shows. What sort of mileage has the car you are inspecting done? Many Ferraris do only about 6,000 miles a year, as fun cars. A high mileage (for its year) 308 should be distrusted.

Insist on a good long trial run before making a choice, as a 308 is an entirely different animal when warm than when cold. When cold, for instance, the Koni dampers rattle, which is normal, but at any speed the ride is hard and joggly. A softer ride, therefore, indicates damping which is on the way out.

Cold starting is tricky enough at the best of times in poor weather, but have the start demonstrated by the current owner. How does it start when hot? There should be no hesitation.

308's having a mid (behind driver) engine and a front radiator, sometimes suffer from cooling system leaks; this car be checked out when the system is thoroughly cold and thoroughly hot. Bubbling noises in the system usually mean low water rather than a blown head gasket.

The engine needs regular attention. Cam drive belts have to be changed at 24,000 miles, and valve clearances should be re-set at that time, or certainly by 36,000 miles. A clattery engine usually denotes wear in the valve gear, which if neglected can lead to worn cam profiles, and necessitate new cams. The bottom end, if kept full of nice clean oil, seems to be bomb-proof. Clutches, by the way, last no more than 24,000 miles, often even less. Gearboxes and final drives, however, are o.k. if not abused from cold. Lack of second gear synchromesh may be the first signs that this has been disregarded. Carburettors which have been "adjusted" by amateurs lead to poor performance and heavier fuel consumption; properly set, the system is reliable and the engines smooth.

Look for worn wishbone bushes (front and rear), which cannot be lubricated, and for disc pad wear (particularly at the rear) as it is not desirable to reskim the ventilated discs if you have the misfortune to wear pads out to their back plates. Not more than 15,000 miles, often much less, can be expected from the pads. A 308 should do better on the expensive tyres - 15,000 miles being normal, though this could be very much less depending on usage.

In summary, a secondhand 308, either the 2 + 2 or the two-seater, can be a very enjoyable but expensive indulgence. Like a Rolls Royce or any other really exotic car, however, it must be serviced and maintained lovingly and meticulously. You must choose such a car, or you will pay dearly afterwards. Indeed you will have to pay over the odds (perhaps up to £1,000 over the price guide we give) for a really good one. Even then, the depreciation, when you come to sell the car, will be very high. As to insurance, it is best not to enquire if you have a sensitive disposition. But then, as a Ferrari lover, you will already have come to terms with the fact that a true Italian love affair comes from the heart and never considers practicalities.

# FERRARI 308, 328 AND MONDIAL CHASSIS NUMBERS AND REVISIONS
## (Chassis numbers for right-hand drive cars from 1974 onwards plus the details of any revisions)

| Model | Year | Chassis No. | | Remarks |
|---|---|---|---|---|
| | | 27261 | June 1979 | Recessed clock, oil and temperature gauges |
| | | 28393 | July 1979 | Gas struts on rear lid |
| | 1980 | 30379 | Jan 1980 | Continued |
| | 1981 | 34347 | Mar 1981 | Last GTB version. Replaced by GTBi |
| Ferrari 308GTBi | 1981 | 35257 | Mar 1981 | Bosch K Jetronic fuel injection. Interior trim changed |
| | 1982 | 40031 | Jan 1982 | Continued |
| Ferrari 308GTBQv | 1982 | 43247 | Oct 1982 | Quattrovalvole version introduced. Replaced GTBi |
| | 1983 | 44649 | Jan 1983 | Continued |
| | 1984 | 48759 | Jan 1984 | Continued |
| | 1985 | 55375 | Jan 1985 | Continued |
| | | 58255 | Aug 1985 | Quattrovalvole discontinued. Replaced by 328GTB |
| Ferrari 328GTB | 1986 | 60841 | Jan 1986 | Introduced Oct 1985, available Jan 1986. Body similar to 308GTB but with grille now enclosing rectangular light units incorporating fog, side and flasher units set in moulded bumper. High rear aerofoil optional. |
| | 1987 | 68375 | Jan 1987 | Continued |
| | | 73059 | July 1987 | Interior door handles changed |
| Ferrari 308GTS | 1978 | 23419 | Feb 1978 | Spider version of GTB. First cars imported had detachable section in roof. |
| | 1979 | 26635 | Jan 1979 | Continued |
| | | 28393 | Jun/July 79 | Modified as 308GTB. See above |

# FERRARI 308, 328 AND MONDIAL CHASSIS NUMBERS AND REVISIONS
## (Chassis numbers for right-hand drive cars from 1974 onwards plus the details of any revisions)

| Model | Year | Chassis No. | | Remarks |
|-------|------|-------------|---|---------|
| | 1980 | 30119 | Jan 1980 | Continued |
| | 1981 | 32047 | Mar 1981 | Last GTS version. Replaced by GTSi |
| Ferrari 308GTSi | 1981 | 34995 | Mar 1981 | Bosch K Jetronic fuel injection. Interior trim changed |
| | 1982 | 40171 | Jan 1982 | Continued |
| Ferrari 308GTS Qv | 1982 | 43147 | Oct 1982 | Quattrovalvole version introduced. Replaced GTSi |
| | 1983 | 44437 | Jan 1983 | Continued |
| | | 47341 | Sept 1983 | Continued but with colour-keyed windscreen surround |
| | 1984 | 48799 | Jan 1984 | Continued |
| | 1985 | 55187 | Jan 1985 | Continued |
| | | 58751 | Aug 1985 | Discontinued. Replaced by 328GTS |
| Ferrari 382GTS | 1986 | 60765 | Jan 1986 | Introduced Oct 1985, available Jan 1986. Styling details as for 328GTB |
| | 1987 | 67837 | Jan 1987 | Continued |
| | | 73021 | July 1987 | Interior door handles changed |
| Ferrari Mondial 8 | 1981 | 33737 | Aug 1981 | Introduced. 2+2 coupé body. Digiplex electronic ignition and Bosch K Jetronic fuel injection. Leather upholstery standard. Digital displays, air-conditioning standard. Electric windows, central locking |
| | 1982 | 39137 | Jan 1982 | Continued |
| Ferrari Mondial Qv | 1982 | 42955 | Aug 1982 | Quattrovalvole version introduced. Replaced Mondial 8 |

# FERRARI 308, 328 AND MONDIAL CHASSIS NUMBERS AND REVISIONS
## (Chassis numbers for right-hand drive cars from 1974 onwards plus the details of any revisions)

| Model | Year | Chassis No. | | Remarks |
|-------|------|-------------|---|---------|
| | 1983 | 44363 | Jan 1983 | Continued |
| | | 46521 | Jun 1983 | Minor interior changes, e.g. box with lid replaced soft pocket between seats. Cabriolet version introduced into USA in September |
| | 1984 | 48873 | Jan 1984 | Continuation of Qv version |
| | | 50513 | June 1984 | Cabriolet version introduced |
| | 1985 | 55207 | Jan 1985 | Qv 2+2 version continued |
| | | 53355 | Jan 1985 | Cabriolet version continued |
| | | 58619 | Sep 1985 | Qv 2+2 version discontinued. Replaced by 3.2 Mondial |
| | | 58913 | Sep 1985 | Cabriolet version discontinued. Replaced by 3.2 Cabriolet |
| Ferrari 3.2 Mondial | 1986 | 61047} 62561} | Jan 1986 | 2+2 and Cabriolet versions introduced Oct 1985, available Jan 1986. Styling generally similar to 328GTB/GTS. Rear wings house radiator grilles. Circular rear light clusters |
| | 1987 | 67973} 68847} | Jan 1987 | 2+2 and Cabriolet versions continued |

# Dino 308 GT4

*Design analysis of latest small Ferrari*

**by Edward Eves**

*Above: The 308 has more angul[ar]
lines than its predecessor and h[as]
outward as well as mechanic[al]
similarities with its competito[rs]
from Lamborghini and Maser[ati]*

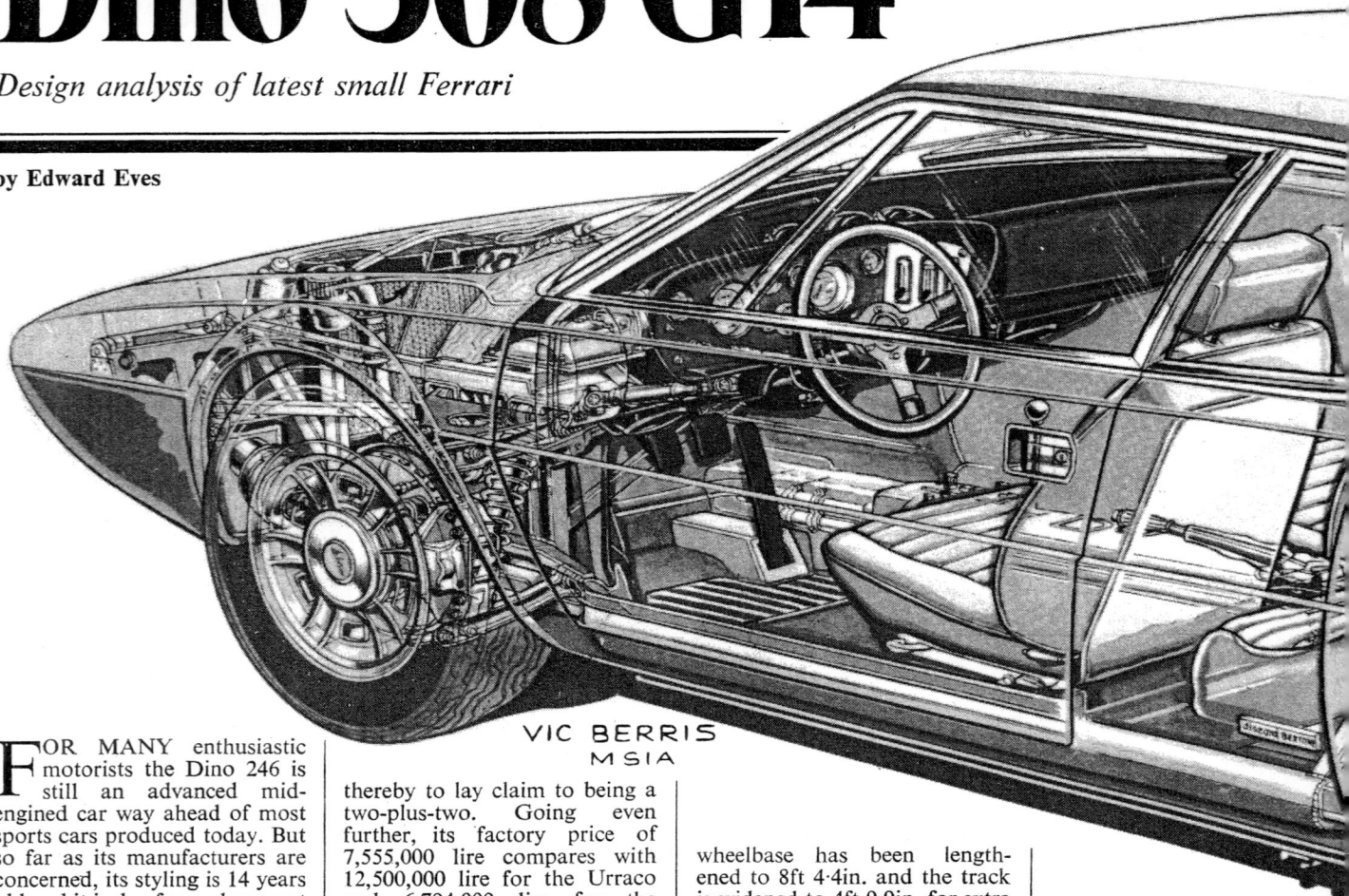

VIC BERRIS
M SIA

FOR MANY enthusiastic motorists the Dino 246 is still an advanced mid-engined car way ahead of most sports cars produced today. But so far as its manufacturers are concerned, its styling is 14 years old and it is due for replacement to contend with newcomers in the same category like the Lamborghini Urraco and the Maserati Merak which in their turn were aimed at nibbling away some of the Porsche 911 market. So it is consequently no coincidence that the 246 replacement, the Dino 308 GT4, is a V8 three-litre car with the engine set behind the passenger compartment and having two front seats and two vestigial rear seats,

thereby to lay claim to being a two-plus-two. Going even further, its factory price of 7,555,000 lire compares with 12,500,000 lire for the Urraco and 6,704,000 lire for the Porsche 911.

In general configuration the Dino 308 GT4 is like the earlier 246 with a transverse vee engine mounted behind the passengers and driving through a unitary 5-speed gearbox. The radiator is mounted in a duct at the front of the car, the cooling water reaching the engine via tubes housed in a duct down the middle of the frame. To accommodate the rear seats, the

wheelbase has been lengthened to 8ft 4·4in. and the track is widened to 4ft 9·9in. for extra stability. An advantage of the transverse engine layout is that a luggage boot is made possible. Ferrari, delightfully, quote its capacity as 250 litres or 55 Imp gallons. We make this 8·8 cu. ft. There is also storage for small articles under the "bonnet" and, of course, on the back seat which is hardly ever likely to be inhabited by human beings because of the absence of leg room.

While the Dino 308 GT[4] has come to supersede t[he] 246, the Ferrari Boxer [] replaces the front-engined Da[y]tona, a fact which should co[n]firm that the arrangement h[as] some merit.

At the risk of dwelling t[oo] long on comparisons the Di[no] 308 GT4 weighs 1,365[kg] (3,009lb) dry, has a 2,927 c.[c] 90deg. V8 engine developi[ng] 250 bhp (DIN) and is claimed []

40

the makers to be capable of 148 mph. The Urraco weighs 1,308kg (2,884lb), has 220 bhp (DIN) from a 2,463 c.c. V8 and a maximum of 143 mph. The Merak weighs 1,320kg empty, has 195 (DIN) from a 2,965 c.c. V6 engine and is claimed, optimistically we think, to achieve 149 mph. The Porsche 911, in Carrera form, has 210 bhp (DIN) to play with, weighs 1,075kg (2,370lb) and has a tested maximum of 149 mph. Its main attraction today in the face of stern market opposition is its fine competition record and impeccable finish.

Although the styling of the Dino 308 GT4 is new, the body is superimposed on a derivation of the 246 chassis. The main novelty is the 90 degree V8 engine. Ferrari have built engines with all multiples of two cylinders from two to twelve. Among these are inevitably a few V8s. The 81 × 71mm 308 unit is not derived directly from any of these, being designed to be made on the Fiat Dino production

machinery. However, it naturally benefits from the experience gained from engines as potent as the 248/SP and 268/SP. Indeed it has the 71mm stroke first found on the Dino 206S and which has since figured prominently on the GT engines. Just for the record the 206S had cylinder dimensions of 77 × 71mm, giving a capacity of 1,985 c.c.

Belt driven camshafts are possibly the most important innovation of the Dino 308 GT4. They are just pre-dated in production, at Maranello by the Boxer BB which is the first production Ferrari to be so fitted. These cog belts are the glass fibre reinforced type and Ferrari's decision to use them was no doubt influenced by the research initiated at Fiat by Aurelio Lampredi, Fiat's chief engine designer, who was for some years Ferrari's top engine man. Their use not only makes for a quieter engine, since they eliminate chain thrash, but they also make for a simpler, cheaper engine since they eliminate the complication of coring and

*Above: The cockpit is laid out in typically neat Ferrari style. Gated gearchange is to the right of the central tunnel Right: Very limited space under front "bonnet". Spare wheel is strictly of the get-you-home variety. Battery lives in right-hand front wing*

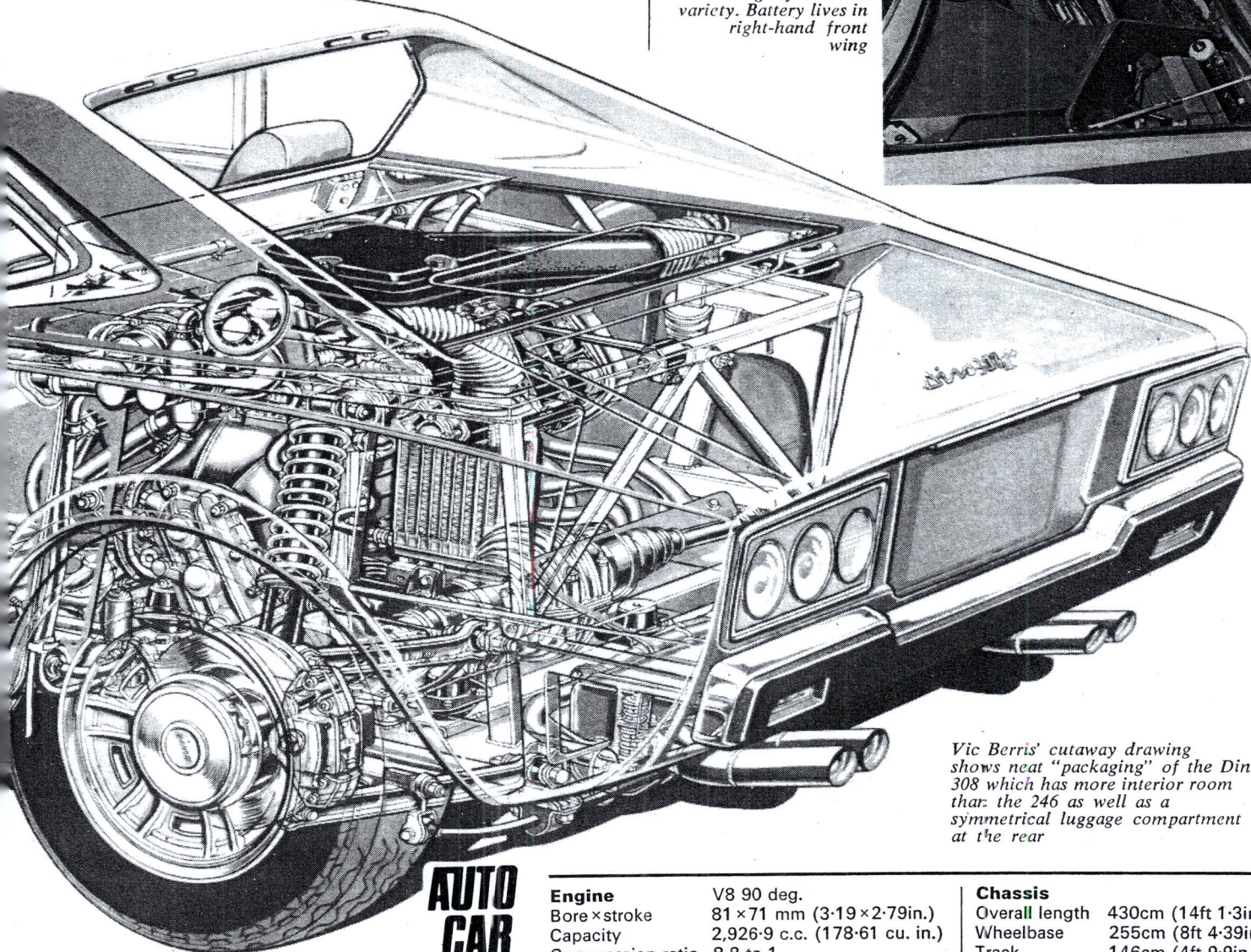

*Vic Berris' cutaway drawing shows neat "packaging" of the Dino 308 which has more interior room than the 246 as well as a symmetrical luggage compartment at the rear*

**AUTO CAR** COPYRIGHT

| Engine | |
|---|---|
| Bore × stroke | 81 × 71 mm (3·19 × 2·79 in.) |
| Capacity | 2,926·9 c.c. (178·61 cu. in.) |
| Compression ratio | 8·8 to 1 |
| Power | 250 bhp (DIN) at 7,700 rpm |
| Max. torque | 210 lb. ft. at 5,000 r.p.m. |

Engine V8 90 deg.

| Chassis | |
|---|---|
| Overall length | 430cm (14ft 1·3in.) |
| Wheelbase | 255cm (8ft 4·39in.) |
| Track | 146cm (4ft 9·9in.) |
| Height | 121cm (3ft 11·6in.) |
| Weight (dry) | 1,365kg (3,009lb) |

# Dino 308 GT4

casting timing cases. There is also some weight saving which is partly offset by the need to provide belt guards. A drawback is that cog-belt drive to the camshaft adds a few millimetres to the overall length of an engine compared with chain or gear drive.

The crankcase and cylinders are the heart of any engine. In common with all other Ferraris – except the very first Fiat-based ones – the combined crankcase and block of the 308 is a light alloy casting with inserted cast-iron cylinder liners. One of its main features is the deep crankcase extended well below the lowest throw of the crankshaft in the interest of rigidity. It also makes for a simplified sump joint. Further rigidity is imparted by webbed main-bearing partitions. Light alloy bearing caps secured by studs and located by ring dowels retain the crankshaft. The cylinder liners are located in the usual Italian manner in deep spigots – a little less than half the length of the liners – raised from the floor of the cylinder water jackets. Contrary to the trend towards open-deck blocks, the top of the water jacket is closed. Counterbores are machined in the top face to take substantial flanges formed on the rims of the liners. To keep the length of the engine down, adjoining liners have mating flats machined on the flanges. On assembly the liners are pressed into the block and

either side of the centreline. It has also been necessary to set the single sparking plug to one side between the valves. Valve throat diameters are 37mm and 34mm respectively, suggesting that while filling will be good at high speeds low speed torque might not be so good as with an engine having smaller diameter tracts.

In common with the 246 the heads are designed for production with all machined surfaces square or parallel to the head face and the tappet guides machined directly in the head. Apart from simplifying machining of the port faces this makes for a bigger head with water space right round the parts. Incidentally it is interesting to compare this head with that of the Fiat 124S which has angled port faces and no water space beneath the exhaust – or inlet – parts. The flat top face of the Ferrari head permits the use of a single cam cover but no attempt has been made to combine it with the camshaft bearing caps. These are separate so that the cover can be removed for access to the tappets without disturbing the camshafts. The use of Fiat disc shims in the tops of the bucket tappets allows clearances to be set without disturbing the valve gear.

Like the Boxer engine the camshafts cogbelts are driven at less than engine speed through intermediate gears driven off the nose of the crankshaft. This

arrangement not only makes for a bigger driving cog – better because the belt flexes less and therefore runs cooler – but provides power take-offs from idler gears to drive the oil pump and water pump. The belts are tensioned by jockey pulleys operating in the slack sides of the belts. The inlet valves start to open 34 deg. before TDC and are fully closed 46 deg. after BDC. The exhausts open 36 deg. before BDC and close 38 deg. after TDC.

The flow of water through the engine from the radiator outlet is first of all into the exhaust side of the head and then to the inlet side and into the water jackets, thus ensuring a regular heat gradient through the engine. Mixture is provided by four, double-choke Weber 40 DCNF carburettors mounted on short, cast manifolds. Water heated hot spots are provided, drawing hot water from the return pipe running along the cleavage between the cylinders.

An unusual two-breaker Marelli distributor determines the firing time. One set of points is set for the idling condition with minimum emissions and fires the plugs at after top dead centre. The other set is brought in by a micro switch in the throttle linkage when the accelerator is depressed and is advanced by 6 degrees. This way a wide ignition spread is achieved by simple means. A similar set-up is to be found on late models of the 246.

The transmission layout is identical with that of the 246, the only difference being in the choice of gear ratios. In effect

the engine sits on a large, box-like casting which is divided by a transverse partition. The engine oil is contained in the section forward of the partition while the five-speed two-shaft transmission and final drive are housed in and about the rear partition. Power is transmitted down from the clutch to the gearbox through three step-down gears contained in an elegant little case which appears hardly big enough to house a motor cycle magneto drive. Nevertheless, due to careful design and suitable choice of both angles, these transfer gears are remarkably trouble-free as has been proved in the Dino 246. A quill shaft takes the drive from the transfer gears into the box, absorbing torsional vibrations in the process.

Advantage is taken of the ample room in the gear casing to provide really substantial Porsche synchromesh. The helical gear for the final drive is located in the middle of the second motion shaft and is steadied by a bearing in a partition down the middle of the box. Drive out to the wheels is by way of solid drive shafts with Birfield-Rzeppa constant velocity joints, the inboard ones being the sliding type. Maximum speeds in the gears are given as 41 mph, 59 mph, 83 mph, 113 mph and 148 mph. Under favourable conditions the engine peaks at 7,400 rpm, which is equivalent to 156 mph.

Speeds of this calibre call for brakes and tyres of the highest order. Ventilated discs – 10½in. front and 10¾in. rear – are fitted outboard on all four wheels,

*Right: The Dino's four-cam V8 plus transmission and ancillaries (like the air conditioning unit) make a compact and neat assembly which weighs 640lb*

the tops of the liners ground to a common height of a few thousandths of an inch proud of the block. This device, also used by Alfa-Romeo and Lamborghini, gives the head gasket a good nip at the fire joint.

Although the belt driven camshafts are a breakaway for Ferrari the rest of the head design is thorough rather than original. There has been no move to use four instead of two valves per cylinder as is the British trend on even modestly priced cars, so the valves are inclined at the "old fashioned" angle of 46deg. Valve angle is defined by the size of valves the designer wanted to use, which in this case was 42mm inlet and 38mm exhaust. To get them into an 81mm head they had to be canted over to 23 degrees on with the handbrake working on small drums cast in with the rear discs. Dual hydraulic circuits, split front to rear, are provided, actuated by a tandem master cylinder. A Bonaldi vacuum servo provides assistance to apply hard, non-fade pads. The ATE calipers are of the two spot type and a balance valve sensitive to rear suspension height is provided to prevent rear wheel locking when braking hard.

Michelin 205/70 VR14, XWX tyres are recommended with Goodyear Grand Prix 800 to the same specification as an alternative; they are mounted on Campagnolo light alloy wheels. The spare wheel provided is a small section, get-you-to-the-nearest-garage device stowed in a well behind the radiator duct. The road wheels proper will not fit into this stowage area and in the case of a puncture one motors gently to the nearest garage, presumably stowing the punctured wheel among the children in the back seat.

## Chassis and suspension

The Dino 246 chassis was immensely strong and entirely satisfactory. It was therefore logical that the Dino 308 frame should be built on the same lines. Thus the 308 chassis is based on a square platform of oval tubes set on edge, underneath the passenger compartment. Forwards and backwards from this square are extended parallel members which carry the front suspension and rear suspension and engine mountings. These front and rear extensions are suitably braced by cross members and are braced from the corners of the main perimeter frame by oval tubes of the same section as the main chassis. These little corner braces to the extensions also act to prevent the perimeter frame lozenging. Further to prevent this possibility this central frame is sheeted in with a composite steel and fibre-glass floor. On the 246 this flooring was steel throughout and was backed up by an undertray welded to the upper and lower edges of the perimeter to form a strong box. Not only was this construction heavy but it was also susceptible to condensation and internal rusting. This latest construction on the 308 is not only lighter but is amply strong and avoids the possibility of condensation. Superimposed on this base structure are a box-shaped cage on which the upper and lower front suspension wishbones and coil springs are mounted. At the rear there is an even bigger cage which not only carries the rear suspension but also acts as the frame of the engine compartment. The front member of the cage is the roll over hoop which also acts as the main rear-body-frame. This particular frame is sheeted in to deck level with steel and asbestos and forms the engine compartment fire wall. The upper portion is double-glazed to act as a rear window. Both the front and the rear cages are built up from a square section tube.

The front and rear suspensions are almost identical to those of the 246. It will be recalled that these utilized wishbones pressed from very heavy gauge sheet steel in conjunction with malleable iron wheel carriers. One reason for the high rear frame cage is to provide an abutment for the rear coil springs and shock absorbers which are mounted above the wishbones to make room for the drive shafts and exhaust pipes which also pass between the wishbones in the interests of ground clearance. All the suspension links swing on Teflon lined bushes. At the rear, adjustment is provided for camber and toe-in by eye bolts and locking nuts. The front wheel parts swivel on Ereureich ball joints, doing away with the need for king pins. Steering is by a Cam Gears rack and pinion mounted ahead of the wheels centreline on the front suspension cage.

Although the suspension consists of four pairs of parallel wishbones, geometrically it is very much akin to that of a Formula 1 car. If one analyses the geometry of the rear suspension of a single seater racer of modern design one sees that the upper and lower links are proportioned to reduce wheel camber change to a minimum as the wheel bumps and rebounds. One or other of the links, depending on the designer's fancy, sets and holds the amount of toe-in or toe-out according to the requirements of the tyre and circuit. The long fore and aft radius have no magic quality. They are simply there to transmit braking and power loads to the strong centre section of the monocoque, in the process doing the maximum amount of work for the minimum amount of weight. In a touring car where weight is of not quite such paramount importance it is possible to achieve the same geometry, or better, by more mundane means. The 308 does it with simple fixed length wishbones. Ferrari have a vast amount of data accumulated which they can apply to any suspension problem. Thus they have given the 308 a relatively high – about 10mm – roll height at the back with minimum wheel camber change to keep the tyre treads flat on the road. At the front the roll height is virtually at ground level. This arrangement is similar to that of the 246. In the same context anti-roll bars are fitted back and front.

The 308 is undoubtedly one of the most important sports cars of the present time. Its production is also essential to the wellbeing of Ferrari and it is likely to be produced in far higher numbers than any of its Italian competitors. □

*Below left: The large size of the valves defines the rather old fashioned valve angle, while large diameter inlet ports suggest top-end power rather than low torque. The torque curve confirms this, maximum torque being at 5,000 rpm*

*Below: The Ferrari engineering drawing shows how the length of the 308's engine has been kept to a minimum by using narrow, large diameter bearings. Note the space taken up by camshaft toothed belt drive*

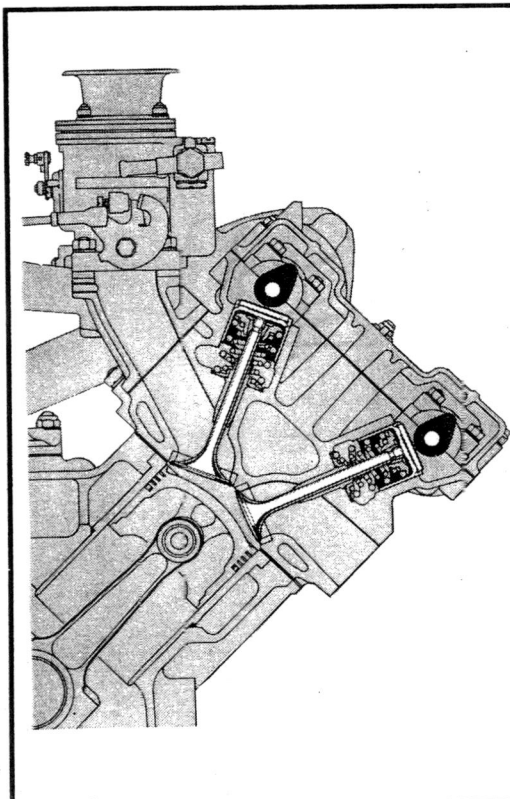

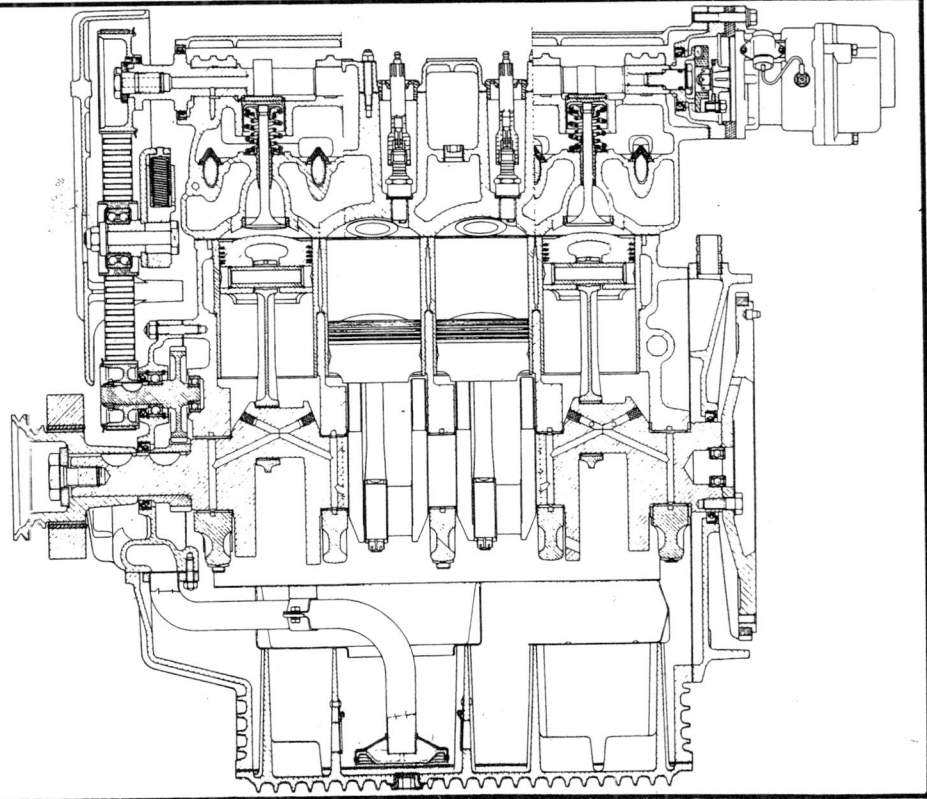

# Ferrari 308 Data File

O f all the Ferraris manufactured since Fiat's takeover of the company in 1969, the 308 GTB and its derivatives have been hailed as the most elegant and stylish of all, balancing an uncluttered simplicity of line with a visual individuality which has endured, largely unchanged, for more than 15 years.

In a nutshell, their development was a key factor which enabled Ferrari to consolidate their march back to economic health after some financially disastrous times in the late 1960s had brought the company to the brink of bankruptcy. The new cars also marked a realisation that the company's model range could only expand and thrive if the standards of build quality were dramatically improved.

Competing against Porsche and like-minded companies in a world market for supercars which was becoming more competitive and demanding by the year, the evolution of the Ferrari 308 and its successors proved that Maranello could offer levels of refinement, build quality and mechanical dependability which had seemed impossible to envisage back in the early 1970s.

*Above: This is a 328 GTS; under the 'bonnet' was room only for a spare wheel.*

*Right: Both 308 and 328 had Ferrari's characteristic round rear lights.*

*Above: The GTB/GTS styling job was given to Pininfarina after the Bertone GT4 had met with a frosty reception from purists.*

*Left: All 308/328s had classy 'star'-styled cast light-alloy wheels.*

## Styling

Ferrari's body styling had traditionally been carried out by Pininfarina when the surprising decision was given to entrust Bertone with the sculpting of the 308 GT4, which appeared in 1973. The resultant sober profile caused a great deal of debate and controversy.

The association between Ferrari and Pininfarina extended back to 1951, and by the late 1980s Sergio Pininfarina had become a director of the Ferrari company. Fiat, on the other hand, had a long-established policy of spreading their outside design commissions to make the widest possible use of the styling talent available.

It has been suggested that this was largely prompted by a desire to prevent any one firm becoming too complacent and comfortable with fat Fiat contracts. Another factor was the Fiat Dino, which was available as a two-seater convertible and a 2 + 2

coupé. The latter was styled by Bertone and proved an altogether more successful confection than the Pininfarina-styled spider. Either way, the 308 GT4 was a one-off contract and the 1975 308 GTB saw the ball firmly back in the Pininfarina court, where it has remained ever since.

Essentially, the body was an update of the original Ferrari Dino of 1967. The main difference was the move away from the flowing curves of the Dino to a slightly harder, more defined, although still smoothly flowing, style. The almost exaggerated curve of the Dino's front wings, for example, was replaced by a lower, flatter, look with pop-up, rather than exposed, headlights.

Originally the body shell was manufactured from glass-reinforced plastic, but that was replaced by steel and aluminium panelling over a tubular frame.

*Below: On both 308 and 328 GTS models a blacked-out, slatted 'sail panel' replaced the GTB's rear quarter-window glass. The flank air intakes fed the engine intake and an oil cooler.*

*Below: On the 328 front side and turn lights were relocated, sensibly, from the bumper strip down into the grille.*

*Below: Seen here with its Targa roof panel removed, the 308 GTS was very popular choice in markets like the USA.*

**Above:** With its three-litre V8 tucked amidships, between the cabin and the rear axle line, the 308 could have a smooth, low bonnet. The front-mounted radiator, however, demanded a grille and prevented the nose from dipping very steeply.

**Left:** The 308 was given neutral handling, although there was enough power to provoke oversteer.

**Below left:** A GTS (spider) variant was added in 1977. Shown here is a later 328 GTS.

## Driving the 308: *every inch a Ferrari*

There are things to complain about with the 308 when you first encounter it: if you're tall, the head room is insufficient; if your left leg is not that strong, you'll have trouble with the clutch; and the steering's surprising weight at low speeds initially makes you wonder if the car really is mid-engined.

As with all Ferraris, everything falls into place once the car is being used at the speeds for which it was designed. When the 308 was being developed, Ferrari's Formula 1 team leader was Niki Lauda and he's credited with having some input into the 308's handling. As a driver Lauda was very fast but very

steady, saving the spectacular until it was needed, and the 308 follows that approach in a way. The 308 is not a nervous-handling car, it's biased initially towards understeer until the extra power that's always on tap is added; in other words the 308 driver can choose how to make the car react. The car's good manners mean that you can even lift off in mid-corner and get away with it, although it's not recommended! Being a Ferrari, of course there are two constants – a noise appropriate to a high-performance car and sufficient power to see the fastest car in the range, the 308 GTBi QV, reach 60 mph in under six seconds.

| PERFORMANCE & SPECIFICATION COMPARISON | Engine | Displacement | Power | Torque (lb ft) | Max speed | 0-60 mph | Length (in/mm) | Wheelbase (in/mm) | Track front/rear | Weight (lb/kg) | Price |
|---|---|---|---|---|---|---|---|---|---|---|---|
| Ferrari 308 GTBi QV | V8, quad-cam, 32-valve | 2927 cc | 240 bhp 7000 rpm | 192 lb ft 5000 rpm | 154 mph 248 km/h | 5.7 sec | 166.5 in 4229 mm | 92.4 in 2347 mm | 57.5 in 57.5 in | 3280 lb 1488 kg | £26,181 (1983) |
| Audi Quattro | Inline-five, overhead-cam | 2125 cc | 200 bhp 5500 rpm | 210 lb ft 3500 rpm | 138 mph 222 km/h | 6.5 sec | 173.3 in 4401 mm | 99.4 in 2525 mm | 56.0 in 57.4 in | 2778 lb 1260 kg | £17,722 (1983) |
| BMW 635 CSi | Inline-six, overhead-cam | 3453 cc | 218 bhp 5200 rpm | 229 lb ft 4000 rpm | 137 mph 220 km/h | 6.9 sec | 187.0 in 4750 mm | 103.2 in 2621 mm | 55.9 in 58.3 in | 3263 lb 1480 kg | £23,995 (1983) |
| Lamborghini Jalpa 350 | V8, overhead-cam | 3485 cc | 250 bhp 7000 rpm | 235 lb ft 3250 rpm | 148 mph 238 km/h | 5.8 sec | 170.1 in 4321 mm | 96.5 in 2451 mm | 59.1 in 61.2 in | 2972 lb 1348 kg | £26,423 (1983) |
| Lotus Esprit Turbo | Inline-four, 24-valve, turbo | 2174 cc | 210 bhp 6500 rpm | 235 lb ft 4500 rpm | 147 mph 237 km/h | 5.8 sec | 171.0 in 4343 mm | 96.0 in 2438 mm | 60.0 in 61.2 in | 2600 lb 1179 kg | £18,913 (1983) |

It's the Ferrari we all love to hate, the 308 GT4. It's the too-angular, too-ugly coupe from the '70s that has dated too quickly to be classic. It's the nightclub owner's Ferrari; the California college rich kid's Ferrari.

Yet it was one of the best-selling Ferraris of its era: so what if it became an instant hate object for the more traditional Ferrari fancier (usually not the person who bought new Ferraris anyway); so what if Bertone, not Pininfarina, built the bodywork; who cared if it didn't have quite the pin-sharp dynamics of the fawned-over 246?

Certainly not the sharp-suited Fiat men running Ferrari in 1974, even less the Gucci-clad rich of Europe and America who were queuing up to buy this new watered-down Dino. Ferrari, like anybody else, had to move the metal. Bye bye tradition, hello blatant niche marketing. It built 3500 GT4s all told — a lot of cars by Ferrari standards.

There's no denying that this was a compromised Ferrari. Compromised styling, compromised packaging, and all in the name of a pair of extra rear seats that offered little more than an aching spine and sore knees.

The shape was by Bertone — its one and only production job for Ferrari. Bertone hasn't worked for Maranello before or since, which says something about the low regard the GT4 has always commanded. Quite why Ferrari

## 'So what if it became an instant hate object for the more traditional Ferrari fancier; so what if Bertone, not Pininfarina, built the bodywork. . . Ferrari, like anyone else, had to move the metal'

decided to forsake Pininfarina as its stylist for the first time in 20 years is unclear. Some say the GT4 was a rejected version of Bertone's Urraco, the other mid-engined two-plus-two he was working on at the time.

Whatever the case, the new Dino GT4 was too hunched and wedgy to be beautiful. The flat-roofed, stub-tailed, short-nosed coupe just didn't have the flowing harmony of Pininfarina's 246. About the only clues to its Dino lineage were the sail panels swooping down from the roof to enclose a vertical rear window. Bertone — who himself drove a GT4 — built the bodies at his Turin factory.

Using a longer-wheelbase, wider-tracked version of the 246 Dino's welded-tube chassis, Bertone squeezed in two tiny, knee-crushing rear bucket seats, which meant placing the front seats well forward, too.

The engine, at least, was an uplifting note: a brand new three-litre V8 mounted behind the seats. Its four camshafts were driven for the first time by two belts, Fiat style, to cut down high-speed thrash. It was Ferrari's first road-going V8: the only lines of ancestry were the Lancia Ferrari D-50 racers of the mid '50s and the Type 158 Formula 1 car of 1964, although it shared its bore and stroke dimensions (81 x 71mm) with the Daytona's 4.4-litre V12.

Sucking through a brace of Weber 40s, this all-alloy unit produced 250bhp at 7700rpm and 209lb ft at 5000rpm and put its energy through a five-speed gearbox. Later, in 1975, there was a poverty 208 GT4, a two-litre 170bhp, 125mph version to beat the Italian displacement tax.

Suspension, steering and braking systems were as the 246 GT — an effective mixture of wishbones and coil springs, high-geared rack and pinion and four big, vented discs.

The car changed little during its seven-year life span. At the same time as the 'Dino' tag was dropped in 1976, the GT4 gained new-style wheels and a bigger front grille — but lost one of its twin distributors.

The GT4 was slightly cheaper than the Jaguar XJ-S in Britain in 1976 (£9442) and performed more or less identically to the four-speed manual Jag. It could manage nearly 20mpg too: who says Ferraris aren't usable?

The GT4 died in 1980, much the same car it had been in 1974. Its replacement, the Mondial, was another controversial four-seater Ferrari.

Imagine a musclebound Fiat X1/9 and you'll get some idea of the GT4's character. You sit well forward, looking out over a blunt bonnet, wedged into a thin-backed, board-hard fake suede seat, edged in leathercloth.

There's a sober set of dials to look at — set into a sensible wraparound matt silver panel — a thick Momo wheel to hold and what look like Fiat parts bin column stalks to operate the wipers, indicators and quick-acting pop-up headlights.

Sensible GT4 owners put their shopping bags, not their offspring, on those jokey rear seats. There's precious little room in the oblong-shaped boot, and that front compartment holds only the spare wheel and radiator.

It's a cumbersome car at low speeds. The steering is heavy, the turning circle poor (39ft) and reverse in the Porsche-pattern 'box is awkward to engage. Second gear just isn't interested until the gearbox oil has warmed up and thinned out. You can see out of the car well enough, at least, so it doesn't feel quite so big and vulnerable in traffic as some exotics.

Out of town, few would be disappointed with the power — both in spread and delivery it's never less than impressively potent — and there's that beautifully instant, pin-sharp throttle response that makes it such a delight.

Yet it doesn't sound too special, this V8; its hollow-sounding belt thrash and metallic growl won't leave your spine tingling and there's no overrun cackle to listen to. It isn't an unpleasant-sounding engine — it has the urgent snarl of a Lotus twin-cam — but somehow it doesn't sound like a Ferrari. At speed it drones boomily into the cabin, too.

The V8 is wonderfully docile, though. The 3136lb GT4 will chug away from a stop happily and vigorously in second gear and you can slip into the admittedly low top (21.1mph per 1000rpm) as early as 40mph and let the car steam away. It's smooth, too, with revs that come easily and sweetly and muscular fourth-gear acceleration that makes progress swift and effortless. Given enough road, a GT4 could run to 154mph; our 11,000-mile example still felt hale and hearty enough to do it.

Consistent weighting of all the controls is what gives the Ferrari its air of high-speed confidence. The steering, brakes, clutch and gearchange all have a similar weighty precision that makes driving the car quickly and properly quite natural. The closely set intermediates snick through the spring-loaded gate with ego-stroking precision; the clutch bites hard and positively, if a little jerkily until you are used to its ferocity.

Power on, the Ferrari — sitting on old-fashioned 70-series rubber — is neutral in its handling, nimble and neat. Try harder and it's the front that starts to move first, drifting across the white lines noticeably.

It's then that the steering — normally quick and accurate — comes over all numb and lifeless. It's a curious trait that *Autocar* noticed in its test of 1976: "There would appear to be a slight interference between the suspension geometry and steering geometry for there are conditions of roll and lock that produce 'dead'

patches in the feel of the steering wheel. These might lead the unwary to think that the front wheels had gone light at the onset of under-steer. This is not the case as once through the patch, feel through the rack and pinion system returns."

Sure enough, ease off a little and the feel is back, but it's a disconcerting foible I could do without in car like this.

*Autocar* reckoned sudden mid-corner lift-off — especially in the wet — could have the car spinning, but I didn't investigate those realms of the GT4's behaviour. Normally, the combination of natural mid-engined balance, fine braking power and an unexpectedly supple ride make the GT4 an easy, fast drive.

If you fancy a GT4 then now's the time to make your move. This particular car, in mint condition, was insured for £40,000, but you can buy something very nice for £20,000 and a presentable car for maybe £15,000. The GT4 might not be everybody's favourite Ferrari, but it is the cheapest. ∎

Thanks to Roger Varley for supplying the GT4 photographed here.

Traditionalists hated the hunched Bertone styling, but the 308 GT4 was still a hit in the '70s

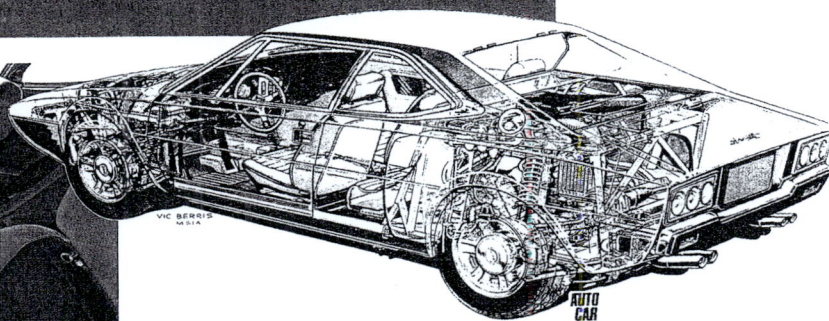

Mid-engined GT4 had Ferrari's first road-going V8: a three-litre unit producing 250bhp at 7700rpm

Cabin is cramped despite two-plus-two design, with board-hard seats, sober dash and cheap switchgear

# ON TOP OF THE WORLD

**The 2+2 Mondial is the 'Ferrari for the family man.' Now with a more powerful engine, how does it shape up?**

# FERRARI MONDIAL 3.2 QV

There is no need to search for the name. The silver horse, rearing up on its hind legs, simply says it all: Ferrari. Park the car in a city street and watch just how many people pause to take a closer look at it. On the open road, and even if you are in no particular hurry, other drivers will make room for the car. And few drivers in GTi-badged hatchbacks will pit their cars against the 270bhp of thoroughbred Italian engineering.

The Mondial first appeared at the Geneva show six years ago, a 2+2 to complement the two-seater (then called the 308GTB). As with all the other current Ferraris, the Mondial has a tubular steel chassis and, like the 328, the body was designed by Pininfarina, although the cars are built at Ferrari's Modena factory.

The original 3-litre V8 engine had two valves per cylinder, but in 1982 the four-valve heads were fitted to make compliance with the US Federal emissions regulations easier. Last year, the capacity was raised to 3.2 litres and the power output increased to 270bhp at 7000rpm. The engine itself is a classic example of how to make a piece of engineering not only work efficiently and sound wonderful but also look the part. The red air intake plenum chamber, with its bright, machined fins, bears that evocative name — Ferrari.

Belt drives are used to the twin overhead camshafts, and the all-alloy block has wet cylinder liners. There is an oil cooler, with its own fan, located behind the air intake just ahead of the right-hand rear wheel. The water radiators, with twin electric fans, are at the front of the car, behind the three-slat grille.

## PERFORMANCE

To anyone who is sitting behind the wheel of a Ferrari for the first time, the prospect of coping with all that potential power might seem a little daunting. But in practice the Mondial is an amazingly easy car to drive, thanks in no small way to the flexibility of that V8 engine and the curiously low gearing.

The Bosch K-Jetronic petrol injection gave first-time starting even when the engine was very hot after a long, high-speed run. Cold starting too, admittedly during some fairly warm weather, gave no problems. But until the gearbox had warmed up a little, it could be difficult to select second gear. The gearchange pattern follows the classic racing type ▶

## TECHNICAL FOCUS

When the 2+2 Mondial first appeared at the 1980 Geneva Show, it was a car with the United States market very much in mind. At that time 35 per cent of Ferrari production went to the States, and the Mondial was designed to meet all forthcoming safety regulations which had just been announced.

The initial engine size was 3-litre, the same as that in the 308GTB, but with Bosch K-Jetro-

nic injection in place of the latter's Weber carburettors. Power output for that engine was 214bhp at 6500rpm. Two years later, the Mondial engine was given new cylinder heads, with four rather than two valves per cylinder — hence the qv for *quattrovalvole*. The power was then hiked to 240bhp. This increase was necessary to keep up with the amount of power being absorbed by the US

Federal requirements on exhaust emissions.

The last change came at the 1985 Frankfurt Show. The capacity was increased to 3.2-litres, with a corresponding boost in power, up to 270bhp.

In addition to the 2+2 coupé version, there is also a cabriolet model. Both cars are designed by Pininfarina, but built at Ferrari's Modena factory.

◄ with first (needed only for starting from a standstill) on its own down to the left and opposite reverse. The pencil-thin, chromium-plated gear lever, with a large, black spherical knob, working in a six-slotted gate, is of a design which has hardly changed since the days of the legendary 250GTO.

It does not take long to realise just how low-geared the Mondial is. Top gear pulls a mere 20.9mph/1000rpm, which means that the car can be trickled around in traffic in this gear, and then rocket up close to a glorious-sounding 7000rpm and 144mph.

Getting the Mondial off the line needed a little care. The fat Michelin 225/55VR16 Michelin TRX rear tyres are reluctant to spin, and unless the clutch is treated carefully the engine revs can be too easily killed. But once the technique has been mastered, the Mondial rockets away. It took just 2.6secs to reach 30mph, with 60 coming up in 6.8secs, 100 in 16.5secs and 130mph in 32.8secs.

The only slightly awkward movement of the gearchange is the dog-leg one from first to second. The others are simply a matter of moving the lever as quickly as you can, with quite a lot of effort needed to overcome the very powerful synchromesh.

A look at the in-the-gears figures shows just what a broad power and torque spread this V8 engine has. The power just comes pouring in, without any of the unseemly, sudden rush which is a feature of so many high-performance turbocharged engines.

The rev counter, which reads to 10,000rpm, is red lined at 7600rpm, but on the test car the rev limiter cut in at 7400rpm. The rev counter also under-read by 7.5 per cent. With its low gearing, it did not take the Mondial any great time or distance to reach its top speed of 144mph, equivalent to 6900rpm, or within a whisker of the top of the power curve.

## ECONOMY

For anyone considering a car in the performance catergory of the Mondial, the cost of the fuel on which to run it will probably not appear very high on the list of priorites. Anything over the 20mpg mark is outstanding, but considering just how heavy the Mondial is, the 16.8mpg we achieved is reasonably good. Much of the test mileage was covered at well over 100mph, so under this country's rather stricter overall speed limit, the average owner could expect to get consumption figures rather better than that.

The 19.8-gallon tank has its filler under an electrically controlled flap on the right-hand rear wing. If the electrics fail, a toggle reached from the engine bay can be used in an emergency. Even when the car is being driven hard, it can be expected to cover around 300 miles between refills, allowing for a couple of gallons in reserve. Ferrari's years of racing experience mean that the Mondial's tank can be filled very easily, without any blow back or bubbling. Over the relatively short test distance, the V8 engine used no measurable amount of oil.

## REFINEMENT

It would be a soulless character who did not revel in the wonderful noise which the Mondial's V8 engine creates when hard at work. Yet even when the rev counter needle is well past the 7000rpm mark, this wonderful piece of Italian engineering never sounds at all stressed. It was built to do just that sort of job.

Yet around town, the car is as docile as one could wish, the engine burbling softly. Its tractability also means that there is no need to go screaming up through the rev range when the traffic lights turn green. Wind noise is very well controlled, and even with the sunroof open, it is

possible to carry on a conversation, albeit with raised voices.

There is some tyre noise, especially when the car is driven over coarse, concrete surfaces. But for a car of such high performance, the noise levels are generally very well controlled.

## ROAD BEHAVIOUR

In a world where practically every other car seems to be nose heavy, the Mondial comes as a refreshing surprise, with 55.4 per cent of its weight being carried over the rear wheels. The suspension follows classic lines — double wishbones front and rear, with coil springs and telescopic dampers. There are also anti-roll bars and rear.

At low speeds, the rack and pinion steering can be quite heavy, especially when parking the Mondial in tight spots. But as speed builds, the heaviness disappears, leaving the driver knowing exactly what the front wheels are doing. Three and a half turns are needed to get from lock to lock, and the turning circle is a rather stately 41½ft. It is when the car is being driven on ordinary roads that the amount of bump steer can be felt, twitching the car slightly off line as it passes over manhole covers and other irregularities. This never amounts to anything serious, and the quickness of the steering makes this behaviour easily countered.

It is to the credit of Ferrari's chassis engineers and the aerodynamicists at Pininfarina that the Mondial feels absolutely rock steady at 140mph, with no need for any obvious air dams or spoilers.

The handling is virtually neutral, with perhaps a hint of understeer. With such a flexible engine, it *is* possible to move the rear wheels off line in a corner, but never suddenly. Despite its size, this is a very easy car to drive quickly. Ride quality is remarkably good, for one might expect over-stiff springing and rock-hard damping.

If there is criticism to be aimed at the braking system, it is that in town it can feel a little over sensitive, almost over-servoed. One soon gets used to being slightly feather-footed to prevent the car from being brought to an unseemly and snatchy halt. It takes only 20lb pedal pressure to achieve 0.36g — that is the sort of retardation on which passengers start to comment. And with just 30lb more pedal pressure, the car was brought up at 1.0g, with the fronts just starting to lock. With the majority of the car's weight over the fat-section rear wheels, it is not surprising that the handbrake, located on the outside of the driving seat, recorded an impressive 0.41g.

As one might expect from a car in this class, the brakes coped with our accelerated fade tests extraordinarily well, hauling the speed down at 0.5g from 95mph 10 times in succession without any problems, apart

**Even the** *relatively 'unsporting' Mondial 2+2 turns heads*

from a slight smell at the sixth stop and a hint of vibration on the ninth.

## AT THE WHEEL

There is certainly nothing spartan or basic about the interior of the Mondial. Cream handstitched leather is used on the seats, facia and door panels. The slim-rimmed steering wheel has three spokes, with the familiar prancing horse motif appearing on the boss.

The instrument panel is mounted quite high so that minimum vertical eye movement is needed to look from road to instruments and back again. The large speedometer — reading 6mph fast at 100mph — is flanked by an impressive rev counter both with easy-to-read figures. Between these and the four smaller dials are the total and trip distance recorders, with a less than one per cent error. The smaller dials are for oil pressure and temperature, coolant temperature and fuel tank contents. The column levers follow a normal pattern, with a short one on the left for indicators. Behind this is the longer one for driving lamps. You cannot, incidentally, flash the Mondial's headlamps without first putting them up. The pedals are offset toward the middle of the car.

On our left-hand-drive test car, the gear lever, with its clearly marked gate, was to the left of the central console. On right-hand drive cars, it is moved to the right. Alongside the gear lever is a row of warning lamps covering such items as screen washer level, coolant level and stop lamp bulbs. Behind these there are the rocker switches for windows, and the locks for front and rear boot lids, engine cover, fuel filler flap and glove locker. This last seems a little unnecessary, as the amount of room provided behind the flap is minimal.

During the test period, we were driving in temperatures of over 27 deg C. But the Ferrari's air conditioning, which is a standard fitting, was barely able to keep cabin temperatures comfortable, even on the coldest setting. This was the one really disappointing feature of the car which is well appointed in so many ways.

## CONVENIENCE

The Mondial is close to 6ft wide with the doors closed, so you need a fairly generous amount of room around the car when they are open. In practice, the angle at which they open is a little restricted and this, combined with the rather high sills, makes entry and exit a little awkward. The front seats are a little on the hard side, and lack much lateral support, a shortcoming noticed particularly when the car was being driven fast on twisting roads.

Rear seat leg and headroom is distinctly on the marginal side — but the children would no doubt appreciate arriving at school in a Mondial. The armrest between the rear seats contains a first-aid kit and conceals the emergency release for the engine cover.

Where the Mondial really does fall down is in the amount of room — or lack of it — for carrying odds and ends inside. The glove locker is practically useless and there are only small elasticated pockets on the doors for the handbook and a small map. The only place to stow cigarettes or sweets is in the small, slippery tray positioned alongside the gear lever.

The front 'boot' is not intended to carry much luggage. The brake servo, air conditioning accumulator and spare wheel take up much of the room. The spare is a 220/55VR390 Michelin TRX front wheel, which can also be used over a limited range on the rear. The main boot is located behind the engine bay, and holds a reasonable amount of luggage for two people.

Access around the engine is tight, but apart from some routine checking of oil and coolant levels, this is not the sort of car on which to indulge in too much DIY work.

It is not until you see someone sitting in the Mondial that you realise just how far forward the seats are located. This in turn means that visibility over that relatively long nose is quite good, making the car easy to place in crowded conditions. But care has to be taken when leaving angled side turnings, for there is a major blind spot created by the thick rear quarter pillars ▶

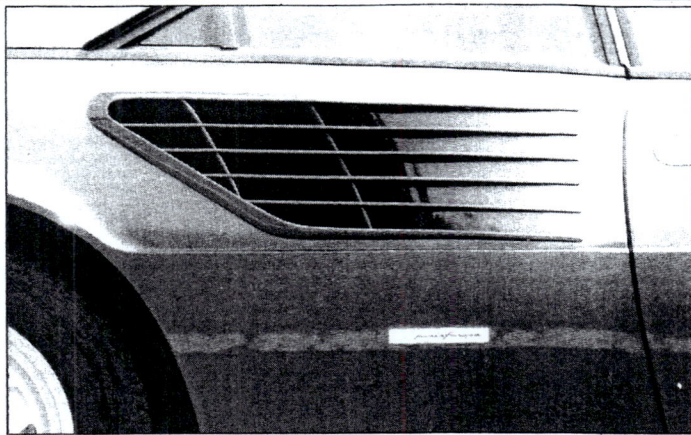

**Cooling air** *for the engine is ducted through inlets*

**To keep** *eye movement to a minimum, instruments are mounted high*

**Tremendous traction** *is provided by Michelin 225/55VR16 tyres*

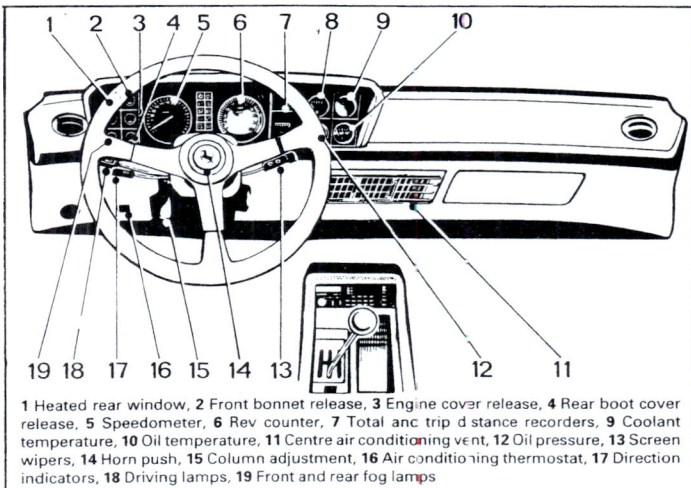

1 Heated rear window, 2 Front bonnet release, 3 Engine cover release, 4 Rear boot cover release, 5 Speedometer, 6 Rev counter, 7 Total and trip distance recorders, 9 Coolant temperature, 10 Oil temperature, 11 Centre air conditioning vent, 12 Oil pressure, 13 Screen wipers, 14 Horn push, 15 Column adjustment, 16 Air conditioning thermostat, 17 Direction indicators, 18 Driving lamps, 19 Front and rear fog lamps

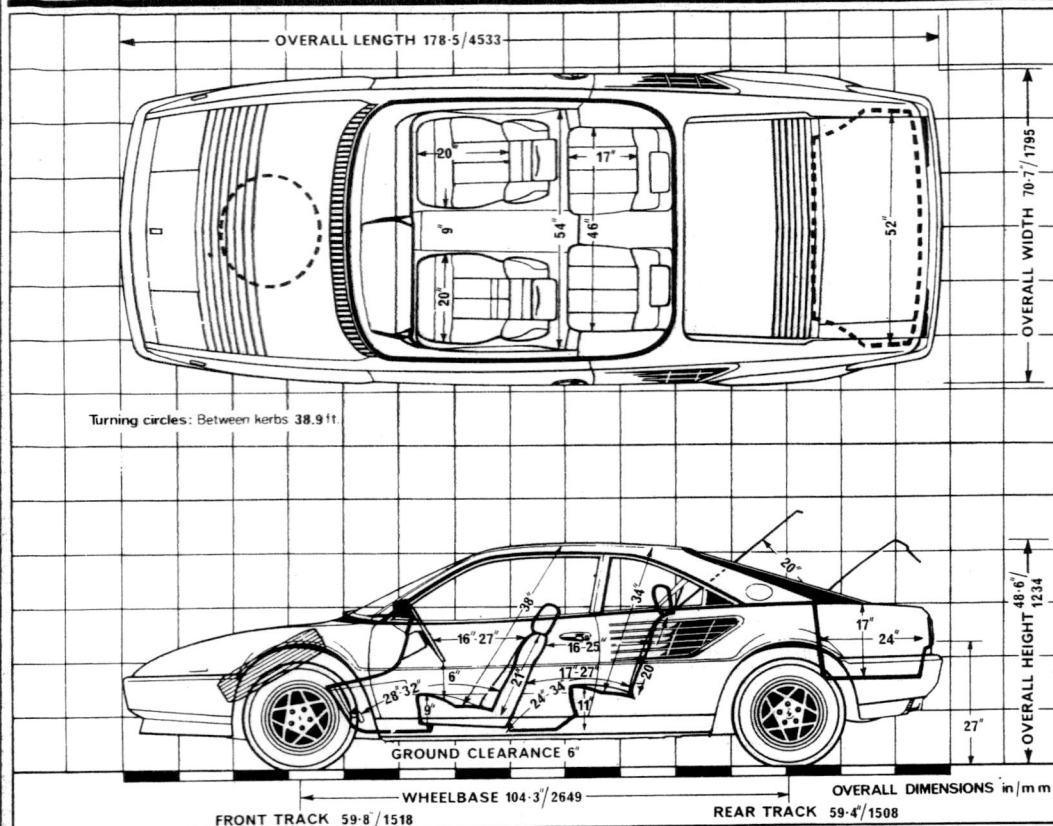

OVERALL LENGTH 178·5/4533

OVERALL WIDTH 70·7/1795

Turning circles: Between kerbs 38.9 ft.

GROUND CLEARANCE 6"

OVERALL HEIGHT 48·6/1234

WHEELBASE 104·3/2649

FRONT TRACK 59·8/1518

REAR TRACK 59·4/1508

OVERALL DIMENSIONS in/mm

## MODEL

### FERRARI MONDIAL 3.2QV

**PRODUCED BY:**
Ferrari Esercizio Fabbriche Corse SpA, Viale Trento Trieste 31, 41100 Modena, Italy

**SOLD IN THE UK BY:**
Maranello Concessionaires Ltd., Crabtree Road, Thorpe Industrial Estate, Egham, Surrey TW20 8RJ

## SPECIFICATION

**ENGINE**
Transverse mid, rear-wheel drive. Head/block al. alloy/al. alloy. 8 cylinders in 90 deg V, wet liners, 5 main bearings. Water cooled, electric fan.
**Bore** 83mm (3.27in), **stroke** 73.6mm (2.90in), **capacity** 3186cc (194.5 cu in).
**Valve gear** 2 ohc, 4 valves per cylinder, toothed belt camshaft drive. **Compression ratio** 9.8 to 1. Marelli Microplex ignition, Bosch K-Jetronic carburettor.
**Max power** 270bhp (PS-DIN) (199kW ISO) at 7000rpm. **Max torque** 224lb ft at 5500rpm.

**TRANSMISSION**
5-speed manual. Single dry plate clutch.

| Gear | Ratio | mph/1000rpm |
|------|-------|-------------|
| Top | 0.919 | 20.90 |
| 4th | 1.244 | 15.44 |
| 3rd | 1.693 | 11.35 |
| 2nd | 2.353 | 8.16 |
| 1st | 3.419 | 5.62 |

Final drive: hypoid bevel, ratio 3.823.

**SUSPENSION**
**Front,** independent, wishbones, coil springs, telescopic dampers, anti-roll bar.
**Rear,** independent, wishbones, coil springs, telescopic dampers, anti-roll bar.

**STEERING**
Rack and pinion. Steering wheel diameter 14.8in, 3.5 turns lock to lock.

**BRAKES**
Dual circuits, split diagonally. **Front** 11.1in (282mm) dia ventilated discs. **Rear** 11in (280mm) dia ventilated discs. Vacuum servo. Handbrake, side lever acting on rear discs.

**WHEELS**
Al. alloy, 7in rims front, 8in rear. Radial ply tyres (Michelin TRX on test car), size 220/55VR390 F, 240/55VR390 R, pressures F34 R35 psi (normal driving).

**EQUIPMENT**
Battery 12V, 66Ah. Alternator 85A. Headlamps 110/220W. Reversing lamp standard. 23 electric fuses. 2-speed, plus intermittent wipe screen wipers. Electric screen washer. Water valve interior heater; air conditioning standard. Leather seats, headlining.

## PERFORMANCE

**MAXIMUM SPEEDS**

| Gear | mph | km/h | rpm |
|------|-----|------|-----|
| Top (Mean) | 143 | 230 | 6840 |
| (Best) | 144 | 232 | 6900 |
| 4th | 120 | 193 | 7800 |
| 3rd | 89 | 143 | 7800 |
| 2nd | 64 | 97 | 7800 |
| 1st | 43 | 69 | 7800 |

**ACCELERATION FROM REST**

| True mph | Time (sec) | Speedo mph |
|----------|-----------|------------|
| 30 | 2.6 | 32 |
| 40 | 3.8 | 42 |
| 50 | 5.3 | 52 |
| 60 | 6.8 | 63 |
| 70 | 8.9 | 75 |
| 80 | 10.8 | 85 |
| 90 | 13.9 | 96 |
| 100 | 16.5 | 106 |
| 110 | 20.1 | 118 |
| 120 | 25.5 | 129 |
| 130 | 32.8 | 140 |

**Standing ¼-mile:** 14.9sec, 95mph
**Standing km:** 27.4sec, 121mph

**IN EACH GEAR**

| mph | Top | 4th | 3rd | 2nd |
|-----|-----|-----|-----|-----|
| 10-30 | — | — | 4.3 | 3.2 |
| 20-40 | 8.5 | 6.1 | 4.0 | 2.9 |
| 30-50 | 7.8 | 5.6 | 3.8 | 2.7 |
| 40-60 | 7.6 | 5.5 | 3.6 | 2.7 |
| 50-70 | 8.1 | 5.5 | 3.7 | — |
| 60-80 | 8.5 | 5.5 | 3.9 | — |
| 70-90 | 9.0 | 5.6 | — | — |
| 80-100 | 9.9 | 5.9 | — | — |
| 90-110 | 10.9 | 6.6 | — | — |
| 100-120 | 11.8 | 8.2 | — | — |
| 110-130 | 13.1 | — | — | — |

**CONSUMPTION**
**FUEL**
**Overall mpg:** 16.8 (16.8 litres/100km) 3.70mpl
*Autocar* constant speed fuel consumption measuring equipment incompatible with fuel injection

| Autocar formula: | Hard | 15.1mpg |
|---|---|---|
| Driving | Average | 18.5mpg |
| and conditions | Gentle | 21.8mpg |

Grade of fuel: Premium, 4-star (97 RM)
Fuel tank: 17.6 Imp galls (80 litres)
Mileage recorder: 1.0 per cent short
**Oil:** (SAE 10W/40) negligible

**BRAKING**
**Fade** (from 95mph in neutral)
**Pedal load for 0.5g stops in lb**

| start/end | | start/end | |
|---|---|---|---|
| 1 | 20-30 | 6 | 30-40 |
| 2 | 20-25 | 7 | 35-40 |
| 3 | 20-30 | 8 | 30-35 |
| 4 | 25-35 | 9 | 20-30 |
| 5 | 25-40 | 10 | 20-30 |

**Response** (from 30mph in neutral)

| Load | g | Distance |
|------|---|----------|
| 20lb | 0.36 | 84ft |
| 30lb | 0.71 | 42ft |
| 40lb | 0.85 | 35.4ft |
| 50lb | 1.00 | 30.1ft |
| Handbrake | 0.41 | 73ft |

Max gradient: 1 in 4
**CLUTCH** Pedal 41lb; Travel 4in

**WEIGHT**
**Kerb** 29.2cwt/3265lb/1477kg (Distribution F/R, 44.6/55.4)
**Test** 32.6cwt/3647lb/165kg
**Max payload** 917lb/415kg

## COSTS

**Prices**

| | |
|---|---|
| Basic | £30,100.00 |
| Special Car Tax | £2508.33 |
| VAT | £4891.25 |
| **Total (in GB)** | **£37,499.58** |
| Licence | £100.00 |
| Delivery charge | £330.00 |
| Number plates | £20.00 |
| **Total on the Road** | **£37,949.58** |
| (excluding insurance) | |
| Insurance group | OA |
| **EXTRAS** (fitted to test car) | |
| Electric sunroof | £903.23 |
| **Total as tested on the road** | **£38,852.81** |

**SERVICE & PARTS**

| Change | Interval | | |
|--------|------|--------|--------|
| | 6250 | 12,500 | 18,750 |
| Engine oil | Yes | Yes | Yes |
| Oil filter | Yes | Yes | Yes |
| Gearbox oil | No | Yes | No |
| Spark plugs | Yes | Yes | Yes |
| Air cleaner | No | Yes | No |

**Total cost** £244.49 £622.50 £244.49 (Assuming labour at £23.00 an hour inc VAT)

**PARTS COST (inc VAT)**

| | |
|---|---|
| Brake pads (2 wheels) front | £36.23 |
| Brake pads (2 wheels) rear | £33.81 |
| Exhaust complete | £1003.95 |
| Tyre—each (typical) front | £124.03 |
| rear | £135.99 |
| Windscreen | £345.00 |
| Headlamp unit | £60.95 |
| Front wing | £233.45 |
| Rear bumper | £621.00 |

**WARRANTY**
12 months/unlimited mileage

**EQUIPMENT**

| | |
|---|---|
| Ammeter/Voltmeter | N/A |
| Automatic | N/A |
| Cruise control | N/A |
| Limited slip differential | ● |
| Power steering | N/A |
| Trip computer | N/A |
| Steering wheel rake adjustment | ● |
| Steering wheel reach adjustment | ● |
| Self-levelling suspension | N/A |
| Headrests front/rear | ●/N/A |
| Heated seat | N/A |
| Height adjustment | N/A |
| Lumbar adjustment | N/A |
| Rear seat belts | ● |
| Seat back recline | ● |
| Seat cushion tilt | N/A |
| Door mirror remote control | ● |
| Electric windows | ● |
| Heated rear window | ● |
| Interior adjustable headlamps | N/A |
| Tinted glass | ● |
| Headlamp wash/wipe | N/A |
| Central locking | ● |
| Cigar lighter | ● |
| Clock | ● |
| Fog lamps | ● |
| Internal boot release | ● |
| Locking fuel cap | ● |
| Metallic paint | ● |
| Radio/cassette | ● |
| Aerial | ● |
| Speakers | ● |

● Standard ○ Optional at extra cost N/A Not applicable † Part of option package DO Dealer option

**TEST CONDITIONS**

| | |
|---|---|
| Wind: | 3-5mph |
| Temperature: | 82deg C (28deg F) |
| Barometer: | 30.1in Hg (1019mbar) |
| Humidity: | 90 per cent |
| Surface: | dry asphalt and concrete |
| Test distance: | 679miles |

Figures taken at 8360 miles by our own staff on the Continent. All *Autocar* test results are subject to world copyright and may not be reproduced in whole or part without the Editor's written permission.

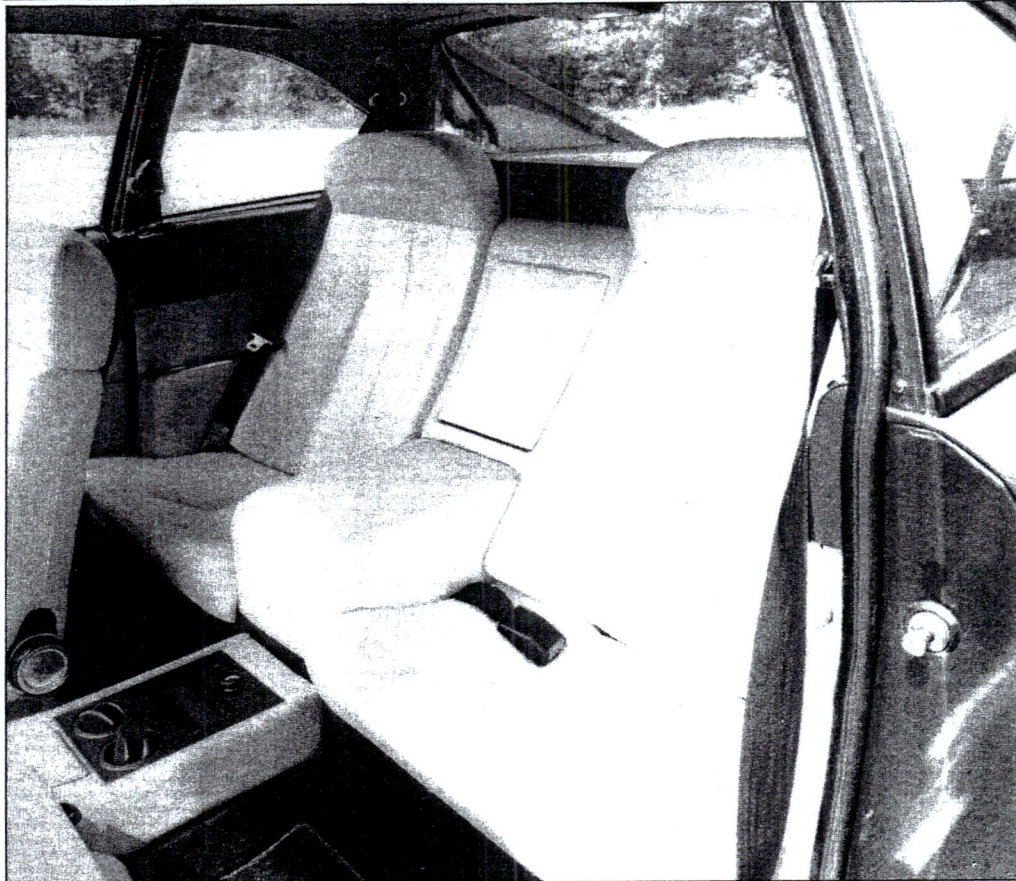

**Rear seat** *leg and headroom is suitable only for small adults or as additional luggage space*

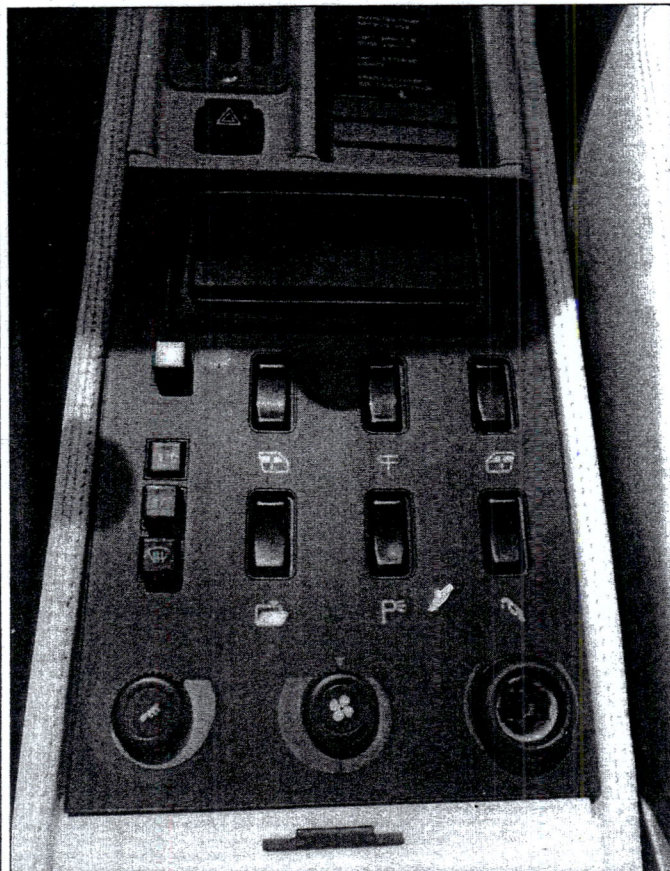

**Central switchgear** *panel houses ventilation/window controls*

## SAFETY

Much of the safety in cars like the Ferrari Mondial starts with the chassis. Give a car of this performance indifferent handling and roadholding and insufficient braking and you have a recipe for disaster. The Mondial's chassis, braking and aerodynamics make it an inherently very stable and safe car. The tubular steel chassis provides immense strength combined with carefully calculated deformation characteristics.

## VERDICT

Among the supercars the name Ferrari and the prancing horse badge still reign supreme, and even the relatively 'unsporting' 2+2 Mondial will turn heads wherever it goes. It is a car with few rivals, perhaps the closest being the Porsche 928S, which provides rather better accommodation and performance in a similar bracket to the Mondial.

Yet looked at in some lights, it is an odd car, with too-low gearing, and indifferent ventilation. Nevertheless, once you have experienced the wonderful noise produced by the V8 engine in full cry, and sat behind that steering wheel, with the power surging in, you can forgive the car for the few detractions it may have. They seem to pale into insignificance as the rev counter needle sweeps past the 7000rpm mark and you slam that gear lever through the gate.

It is a different world of motoring.

# A Buyer's Guide

# Ferrari 308

## The affordable Ferrari? We ask the trade how good the 308 really is and Roberto Giordanelli finds out how well they go

## Background

Keith Bluemel

The 308 GTB made its debut at the 1975 Paris Salon, and complemented the 308 GT4 2+2 model. Both models shared a similar mechanical layout, but the 308GT4 had a slightly longer wheelbase chassis at 2,550mm, against 2,340 mm for the 308 GTB.

After the rather subdued reception that greeted the Bertone-designed 308 GT4, the Pininfarina styling of the 308 GTB drew wide praise from the motoring press and clients alike. One thing not apparent to the casual observer was that the new model marked a departure from standard Ferrari body construction methods employed on the outgoing 246GT, in that, apart from the aluminium front lid, it was totally made of fibreglass, with a very high standard of finish. The use of this material did not last for very long, only until late 1976 for USA market models, and into the middle of 1977 for European versions. The replacement models had steel bodies, but maintained the aluminium front lid. The reasons for the change were allegedly due to slow production time and high accident repair costs. Without resort to a magnet, the easiest way to identify a fibreglass example is to see if there is an indent join line where the roof meets the front screen pillars.

A mechanical difference on the European carburettor-engined examples is that they were fitted with dry sump lubrication, whereas USA examples, and all market versions subsequent to the adoption of fuel

Action photography by Andrew Brown

*Left: Venerable V8 has been around for a long time, this is the 'Quattrovalvole' version.*
*Above: Philip Diamond's car is in excellent condition, according to Mike Wheeler at Talacrest blue 308s are better looked after than red ones.*
*Below: The 308 is one of Pininfarina's most successful designs. Every Italian car enthusiast must have lusted over a red GTS at some time. Spot the odd one out!*

injection, had wet sump lubrication. On all examples the engine was a transverse 90° V8, with a bore and stroke of 81mm x 71mm, initially producing a claimed 255bhp, mated to a five-speed gearbox in unit with the engine and final drive.

At the Frankfurt Salon in September of 1977, after the change to steel bodies in all markets, a targa roofed addition was made to the range, called the 308 GTS. Apart from the black-finished removable roof section, which stowed behind the seats when not in use, these can also be identified by satin black finished hinged louvre panels over the rear quarter windows. During the middle part of 1977 an optional deep front spoiler became available, constructed from fibreglass, as was the standard shallow version.

With emission legislation becoming more stringent in numerous markets, Bosch K-Jetronic fuel injection was adopted in 1980, and the model names changed to 308 GTBi and 308 GTSi. The new, 'cleaner' engines showed a marked drop in power output, particularly those destined for the USA market. Concurrently, changes were made to the interior, and the road wheel size became metric to accept Michelin TRX tyres, with a slight change in the five-spoke design pattern. The question of power output was addressed by the provision of four valve per cylinder heads, and the model name became 308 'Quattrovalvole'. This was presented at the 1982 Paris Salon, and is recognisable by the addition of a slim louvre panel in the front lid to aid radiator exhaust air exit, paired door mirrors with a small enamel Ferrari badge on the case, a revised radiator grille with rectangular driving lights at the extremities, and rectangular side repeater lights. The interior also received some small changes, and cloth seat centres were available as an option to the standard leather. The four valve per cylinder heads brought power output back to a figure similar to the early ➤

*Currently, silver cars are a popular choice*

carburettor cars, and with it a useful gain in performance over the two valve injection models.

In 1976 *Autocar* magazine tested a fibreglass-bodied carburettor car and recorded a 0-60mph time of 6.5 seconds, a 0-100mph time of 17 seconds, and a top speed of 154mph. In 1983 the *Motor* magazine recorded a 0-60mph time of 5.7 seconds, a 0-100mph time of 14.3 seconds, and a top 'speed of 154.5mph, for a quattrovalvole example. Thus it can be seen that the four valve per cylinder heads had the desired performance redressing effect. The QV versions continued in production for three years, until replaced by the 328 models in the Autumn of 1985.

Options available were few over the years. Apart from the previously mentioned deep front spoiler, there was air conditioning, metallic paint, wider wheels, 16" Speedline wheels with Pirelli P7 tyres, and a rear of roof aerofoil on the QV model, although many earlier cars have since had these fitted. For the early carburettor cars there was a sports exhaust system, and high compression pistons plus high lift camshaft option available through Maranello Concessionaires Ltd. There were also special models produced for the Italian market with two-litre engines, due to their tax laws. There was the 208 GTB/S, with a normally aspirated carburettor engine, produced from 1980 to 1982, and then the 208 Turbo, with fuel injection and a KKK exhaust driven turbocharger, which had a production run from 1982 to 1985, when it was replaced by the GTB/S Turbo. Initially the 208 Turbo was only produced in coupe body form, but a targa topped GTS derivative became available during 1983.

# Market Place

## Mike Wheeler - Talacrest

The 308 series has probably introduced more owners to Ferrari ownership than any other Ferrari. They offer an affordable package of good looking cars, with reliable and cost efficient mechanical components, their

maintenance being both reasonably straightforward and not too expensive. The 308s have also proved to be reliable.

Early fibreglass cars had a following with buyers often wanting one because "it won't rust". Wrong - steel sills, A-posts and the steel space frame can succumb to the 'tin worm'. Fibreglass can also star and craze and not all body shops can cope with fibreglass as well as they do with steel. The fibreglass cars often felt loose, so do drive one as they do vary enormously from car to car. The steel bodied cars always felt tighter to me although mechanically much the same, the fibreglass cars apparently were less restricted by emission controls. The carburettor 308 GTBs and GTSs provide something that is missing in the modern cars. The draw of carbs, popping on over-run, all add to their appeal, making the modern cars too clinical and perfect for some. In the case of the GTS this was the last open-air carburettor Ferrari built. Bodies do corrode but not as badly as one would imagine, particularly true of the cars that are garaged badly in damp conditions or, as is often the case, repaired badly. But any that have survived thus far cannot be all bad, after all the youngest is now 19 years old.

The injection cars are often maligned as under powered. Any '80s car with 214bhp is

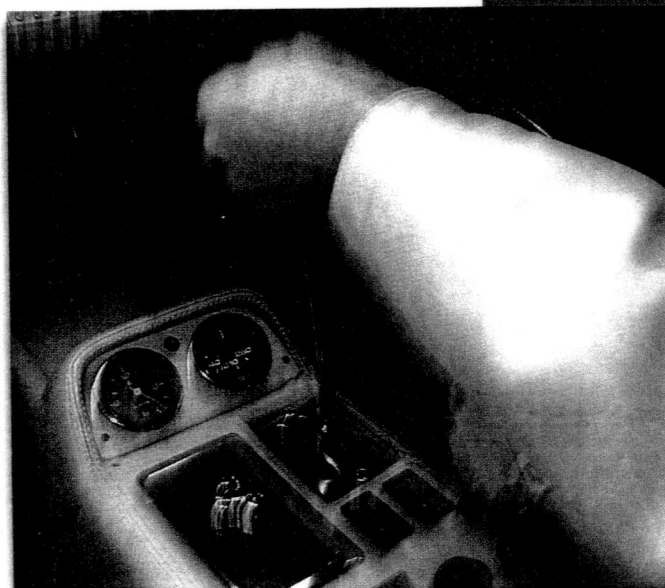

not under-powered - but the lack of the aural buzz along with a loss of power by comparison with the carb cars (a claimed, but rarely seen, 255bhp) resulted in poor sales and the cars today are sold as much on their price as they are on the fact they are a Ferrari. The sheer lack of cars imported has sustained their resale values. The Quattrovalvole or QV restored the 308's image. Power back to 240bhp (much closer to what the carburettor cars actually produced) along with a significant step forward in build quality. Even today a good 308 can be more expensive than its later 328 counterpart. There are two camps - those who like the traditional toggle switches and the sharp front and those who prefer the more modern interior and blunter nose of the 328. In real terms this has meant that 308 values have held and increased steadily and will continue. What Roger Moore and Tony Curtis did for the 246, Thomas Magnum did for the 308.

## Tony Willis - Maranello Sales

Finding a good early 308 GTB is now becoming very difficult. The original glassfibre cars, of which Maranello Concessionaires imported 154 cars out of a total factory production of 712 cars, being especially difficult as the early model with its lighter weight and unique construction made an excellent track car. A larger choice of steel cars became available with 211 GTB and 184 GTS cars imported; however, although these cars are available in greater numbers the appearance of sound cars in the market place is limited.

The rarest, but the most undesirable, model was the two valve injection car with only 42 GTBi and 67 GTSi right-hand drive variants imported. With the introduction of the QV the models regained their performance and 74 GTB QV and 233 GTS QV RHD cars were brought in and these are now the most sought-after.

When the 308 GTB was introduced in 1976 the cost of £10,500 soon rose to £23,500 with the QV. (Today the cost of an eight-cylinder 360 Mocena is £102,000!) When the 308 QV was finally superseded by the 328 GTB the price had risen to £29,500 and this is the top price you would pay today for this version.

## What to look for

Very unlikely to find at an authorised Ferrari dealer, all these cars will be handled by the specialists, who need no introduction as most have been trading for years and probably preparing for test day use or competition in the Maranello Challenge.

These specialists will be well versed in areas of concern such as water pump failures, top end noises, and suspension/steering rack seizures. Get the car properly checked as the ever-present corrosion was a problem despite Maranello Concessionaires offering rust-proofing at point of delivery, technology has moved on.

Most popular in the UK is the GTS version despite the leaks and lack of rigidity, but as the cars are for weekend pleasure who cares, as this is part of the fun of ownership. Do join the Owners' Club to enjoy the car more and feel part of the Ferrari family and understand the value of these models. The difficulty of pricing is such that from £15,000 for the GTBi/GTSi to £25,000 for a fibreglass or QV model is a broad band. Do see, try and inspect every car as what you originally wanted may not be the car you end up with despite a thorough search and reading the excellent Ferrari V3 by Keith Bluemel. But what you will buy is a genuine Enzo-inspired Ferrari, that gave the company something more to be truly proud of and one of the most desirable of Ferraris.

## Driving impressions
### Roberto Giordanelli

The motoring writer gets to see the extremes of the social spectrum. One day it's champagne at £250 per bottle - the next ➤

*This Talacrest car has since been sold, but Mike Wheeler will find you another one!*

The vague controls for heater and air-conditioning need a sympathetic owner. Despite the quirky ergonomics, the 308 has enough style and panache to despatch these faults into insignificance.

The 'old' GTS has that good old-fashioned induction noise and a power delivery that builds progressively and with that deep exhaust note - busy, sporty with an almost metallic rasp. File the heavy clutch and awkward gear-shift under 'character', the yellow badge in the middle of the 3-spoke Momo steering wheel says it all. The open topped GTS has some extra strength built into the chassis. The taller sill section is an obvious one. 308s handle well even by today's standards. Understeer soon gives way to big oversteer. The seats hold you well as you twirl the non-assisted (3.25 turns) steering to correct the sliding XWX Michelins (205/70x14).

Less powerful but newer, the GTBi QV feels no slower. Both manage 6.5 seconds for the 0-60mph yardstick, with about 150mph top speeds. The QV motor builds progressively but at 5,000rpm it finds more urgency despite its maximum power being produced 600rpm lower. With a closed rigid body and its more modern (but inconveniently metric) tyres sizes (Michelin TRX 220/55 VR 390) grip and chassis behaviour were notably stronger with the GTB. Sudden engine braking brought about by lifting off whilst cornering very hard could induce some lift-off oversteer (worse on the GTS). Neither car had ABS. Although neither car has a glove box, the rear boot is a useful size. There is no reason why you could not use a 308 as a track day car as well as your daily transport.

## Verdict

Great looks, rewarding handling, lusty engines, good investment, glorious heritage, bad sitting position - better than giving the money to the barman. ∎

it's half a lager with the Editor. Then there are people out there who spend over £100 per week (£15 per day) drinking in pubs. A financial commitment sufficient to finance the £30k loan for a rather nice 308 Ferrari.

The 308 does look right, and that alone is a good enough reason to own one. From its 1975 Paris launch until handing over to the 328 in 1985, the 308 - in its many guises - took Ferrari into a semblance of mass-production. Here we test two examples: a silver 308 GTS (W-reg Jan 81) and a blue 308 GTBi QV (Y-reg 82/3). Both are fitted with four-cam transversely mid-mounted alloy three-litre engines. The older silver car has two valves per cylinder, four twin-choke Weber DCNF carbs and is rated 255bhp at 7,600rpm. The slightly younger blue GTBi QV has four valves per cylinder, Bosch K-Jetronic injection and is rated lower at 240bhp at 7,000rpm. Power output had dropped, as fuel injection became necessary to meet emission regulations. Quattrovalvole engines boosted power from the 214bhp of the first injection (two valve) motors up to a more acceptable 240bhp.

A Pininfarina classic if ever there was . . . Walking up to the 308 you take in the sculpture and note how this is one of those very rare automotive shapes that is difficult to fault. The 308 cannot be caught out with the equivalent of a 'bad hair day'. It looks good from any angle. Your first physical contact with the Scaglietti sculpture is finger against

door handle. A cheeky black curl of a lever tucked up against the B-post. Inside the 'before-its-time' car, the dash design gives the game away with its boxy '70s styling and quirky switchgear.

The 308's sitting position has often provoked comment about primate-shaped Italians - try any similar quasi-racist stereotypical observation elsewhere and you would be breaking the law. The 'too-far-away-wrong-angle' steering and the 'too-close' pedals are a result of lazy and optimistic designers trying to have their cake and eat it. The 'big interior space' cake and the 'short overall length' cake are the same cake. Engine position, screen rake, front wheel arch intrusion and steering rack position have more influence than 0.001% of Neanderthal throwbacks in the population. The ergonomic disaster continues with a long, heavy clutch pedal. Sit close in order to master the steering and your head nears the sun visor. Cranking the back-rest forward goes some way to counter the non-adjustable column.

| PRODUCTION HISTORY | | |
|---|---|---|
| MODEL | YEAR | TOTAL |
| 308 GTB | 1975 to 1980 | 2,897 |
| 308 GTS | 1977 to 1980 | 3,219 |
| 308 GTBi | 1980 to 1982 | 494 |
| 308 GTSi | 1980 to 1982 | 1,743 |
| 308 GTB QV | 1982 to 1985 | 748 |
| 308 GTS QV | 1982 to 1985 | 3,042 |
| 208 GTB | 1980 to 1982 | 160 |
| 208 GTS | 1980 to 1982 | 140 |
| 208 GTB Turbo | 1982 to 1985 | 437 |
| 208 GTS Turbo | 1983 to 1985 | 250 |

*Giordanelli in evaluation mode*

# Ferrari 308 GT4

## Unloved for decades, the 308 GT4 is finally being recognised as one of Maranello's mid-engined greats

Report by Chris Rees
Photography Michael Ward
Feature sponsored by Superformance

Gawky, rust-prone and – until recently – entirely unfancied, the 308 GT4 has long been the runt of Ferrari's mid-engined litter. Famously the only regular production Ferrari ever designed by Bertone (Marcello Gandini, in actual fact), the GT4 has always been viewed as the ugly duckling to Pininfarina's 308 GTB swan.

But enthusiasts – especially those with fond memories of the 1970s – have recently been flocking to the GT4, appreciating its shape and its super-sweet drive afresh, and finally recognising it as one of the greatest overlooked Ferraris of all time. As a result, prices have truly skyrocketed from 'Mondeo money' just a few years ago – one example is currently up for sale for £75,000.

Launched in 1973 as a Dino, but soon rebadged as a Ferrari, the 308 GT4 was positioned as a 2+2 sister model for the Dino 246. The 246's wheelbase therefore was stretched by 21cm, but the GT4 kept its all-independent suspension, consisting of wishbones, coil springs, dampers and anti-roll bars.

The GT4 was the first model ever to be fitted with Ferrari's all-new and utterly fabulous 3.0-litre V8 engine. The spec still sounds gorgeous today: all-alloy, two overhead camshafts per bank, four Weber carbs and 255bhp of power. It was mounted transversely in the middle of the car, in situ with the five-speed gearbox.

Another first: this was the first mid-engined Ferrari with 2+2 seating. And unlike many mid-engined rivals,

the GT4 can genuinely seat four, also boasting more generous front-seat accommodation than the two-seater 308, and a very decent-sized boot behind the engine.

This was a popular Ferrari in its day. Of the 2826 308 GT4s made, a fairly high percentage came to the UK (547 examples were right-hand drive). An additional 840 examples of the Italian tax-break 208 GT4 were also sold.

## ON THE ROAD

You may be surprised at just how comfortable the 308 GT4 is. Yes, the driving position is a little odd with its offset pedals and low-set steering wheel, but it feels airy and you're greeted by a glorious-looking aluminium-and-chrome dashboard featuring ideally positioned dials and controls.

Crank up the carb-fed engine and its charisma makes an immediate impact: peppy, rev-happy and guttural, with a whole host of pops and bangs from the exhaust as you rev it. It's lively, too, with strong mid-range pull and a scintillating redline of 7600rpm. You can blissfully move up and down the gearbox, the exposed gate with dogleg first delivering superbly slick changes, albeit with a pretty heavy clutch action. The GT4's at its best when you short-shift through the 'box and let the wave of torque carry you onwards, but it's equally great as a cruising machine on the motorway. For the record, the GT4's top speed is 155mph and the 0-60mph sprint takes 6.4 seconds.

What about handling? Here's the great news: the GT4 is one of the sweetest and best balanced mid-engined cars of its era, and arguably the best-handling mid-engined Ferrari until the F355. It's very much at home on twisty A-roads, and totally trustworthy on the limit. The high profile of the 205/70 VR14 tyres makes the initial turn-in a little indistinct, but once you've settled into a corner, you really feel what's happening, thanks to excellent feedback through the steering wheel. Any loss of grip mid-corner can be countered with throttle adjustment to correct the line, and the

GT4 actually makes a surprisingly accomplished track machine.

## ENGINE & TRANSMISSION

The V8 is robust as long as it's treated well and used regularly. The engine bay does get very hot, causing problems for the hoses, headers and sodium-filled valves. Overheating is a definite issue if the radiators clog up, while the electric fans are frequent victims to Ferrari's less-than-reliable wiring.

It's vital that the engine has good oil pressure and that there's no blue smoke (indicating piston ring wear). The two-valve-per-cylinder engine can suffer valve guide wear which leads to high oil consumption, but this is a relatively easy fix. The plugs are also prone to fouling. As for the four Weber carbs, these need proper and careful adjustment, which does take time (and therefore expense, if you're not skilled yourself).

Prompt cambelt replacements are essential, because if the cam belts snap, expect a bill of perhaps £10,000 for a full engine rebuild. Leaking head gaskets can be identified by white emulsion under the oil filler cap. A stainless steel exhaust system is a common (and desirable) fitment.

Check the transmission carefully, too, as there are big bills awaiting if it needs attention (budget £5000 for a full rebuild). The gearbox is often notchy and reluctant to engage, so make sure all the synchromesh works – there should be no crunching through the gears.

## CHASSIS & BODY

The tubular space frame chassis does rust, so check this carefully. The suspension should be greased every two or three years to avoid wear in the ball joints. The rubber bushes tend to wear, so polyurethane ones are popular as replacements. Brakes tend to seize if the car is left unused for a long time, and you should check the brake discs for wear – a replacement set is around £750. Chassis upgrades are generally frowned upon, but modern tyres improve the handling, and uprated brake pads are recommended.

The bodywork is one of the most important things to

# TECHNICAL SPECIFICATIONS
## FERRARI 308GT4

| | |
|---|---|
| ENGINE: | V8 |
| CAPACITY: | 2927cc |
| POWER: | 255bhp at 7600rpm |
| TORQUE: | 210lb ft (285Nm) at 5000rpm |
| TRANSMISSION: | Five-speed manual |
| TOP SPEED: | 155mph |
| 0-62MPH: | 6.4sec |
| WEIGHT: | 1150kg |

heck on any GT4. While the bonnet and boot lid are luminium, everything else is steel, so there's plenty of pportunity for rust to take hold. Pay special attention o the A-posts, rear wheelarches, sills and valances, ut don't ignore the front wings, door hinge surrounds nd the rear window top edge.

The doors should open and shut cleanly with a solid lunk, and there should be no corrosion around their dges. Make sure that the pop-up headlamps do ctually pop up, too. The two fuel tanks are positioned ust ahead of the rear wheels and, if rusty, they cost round £1200 each to replace.

Most cars will have had some paintwork done in the ast, but take care that such work doesn't mask major ssues underneath. Check that the body lines are all risp and sharp. And if you see evidence that a rollcage as been previously fitted, walk away: it's probably een abused as a circuit toy or hillclimb racer.

## INTERIOR

he GT4's standard factory trim was vinyl and cloth, lthough a full leather interior was optional. The 308's lectrics are hardly what you'd call the strongest, with poorly designed fusebox causing lots of problems probably best replaced with an upgraded item). The lectric windows are normally sticky, and if the car has ir-conditioning, expect it to be pretty ineffective.

## RUNNING COSTS

's definitely better to spend more money buying a eally good car than to buy a poor car cheaply, as efurbishment costs are very high. As a result, many iT4 owners have restored their cars piecemeal rather han in one hit – not a problem, but you always need ;ood documentation.

If you use the car regularly, rather than merely toring it, it'll be cheaper in the long run to keep ;oing. Penny-pinching previous owners may well ave skimped on servicing, so beware. By Ferrari tandards, though, this isn't an expensive car to ervice. Expect a major service to cost in the region f £2000, including replacement of the toothed ubber cam belts (which need changing at least very 25,000 miles or two years – ideally more requently). If the clutch is worn (a typical lifespan is 20,000 miles), the parts cost isn't huge, but you'll be :harged up to two days' labour to do it.

The parts situation for the GT4 is surprisingly ;ood. Many items are shared with other cars (such as Fiat X1/9 door strike plates), Maranello carries ots of classic parts, and many items are now being emanufactured.

## VALUES

The days of bargain basement GT4s at £10k are now well and truly over. It's still possible to find cars needing work at around the £20,000 mark but you're much better off with a properly sorted example, and these tend to go for at least £40,000 in today's market. Prices for top-end cars continue to increase, with the very best going for more than £70,000. ∎

### Price Guide
308 GT4, 1980, 50k miles, red, £44,000
308 GT4, 1979, 73k miles, red, £49,980
308 GT4, 1980, 14k miles, red, £75,000

∎ Many thanks to Ferrari specialist Foskers for helping to prepare this buying guide. Contact Foskers at Unit 5 Brands Hatch Park, Kent. Tel: 01474 874777. Web: www.foskers.com

# FERRARI 308, 328 AND MONDIAL CHASSIS NUMBERS

| | |
|---|---|
| Ferrari GTB | Chassis numbers started at 18677<br>Last fibreglass-bodied car was 21289 and first steel-bodied car was 20805.  The last right-hand drive car was 34347 |
| Ferrari GTBi | Chassis numbers started at 31327 and ended with 42617 |
| Ferrari GTB Qv | Chassis number of the first right-hand drive car was 43247 whilst the last right-hand drive car was 58255 |
| Ferrari GTS | The chassis numbers started at 22619 whilst the last right-hand drive car was 32407 |
| Ferrari GTSi | The chassis numbers started at 31309 whilst the last right-hand drive car was 42617 |
| Ferrari GTS Qv | The chassis numbers started at 43147 whilst the last right-hand drive car was 58751 |
| Ferrari Mondial 8 | The chassis numbers started at 31075 whilst the last right-hand drive car was 41359 |
| Ferrari Mondial Qv | The chassis numbers started at 42955 whilst the last right-hand drive car was 58619 |
| Ferrari Mondial Cabriolet | The chassis numbers started at 50513 whilst the last right-hand drive car was 58913 |
| Ferrari 328 GTB & 328 GTS | The chassis numbers started at 60841 (GTB) and 60765 (GTS) |
| Ferrari 3.2 Mondial & 3.2 Mondial Cabriolet | The chassis numbers started at 61047 (right-hand drive 3.2 Mondial) and 62561 (right-hand drive Mondial Cabriolet) |

# FERRARI 348tb
# SPECIFICATION

## ENGINE

| | |
|---|---|
| Location | mid-rear, long mounted |
| Cylinders | 90°V8 |
| Bore x stroke | 85.0 x 75.0mm |
| Capacity | 3405cm³ |
| Induction | electronic multi-point fuel injection |
| Compression ratio | 10.4 to 1 |
| Valve gear | chain and belt driven dohc per bank, four valves/cyl |
| Power | 221kW @ 7200 rpm |
| Torque | 323 Nm @ 4200 rpm |
| Maximum rpm | 7500 |
| Specific power output | 64.9 kW/litre |

## TRANSMISSION

| | |
|---|---|
| Type | 5 speed manual |
| Driving wheels | rear |

## GEARBOX

| Gear ratio | 1000 | kmh rpm | Max speed | At (rpm) |
|---|---|---|---|---|
| First | 3.210 | 10.6 | 80 | 7500 |
| Second | 2.110 | 16.1 | 121 | 7500 |
| Third | 1.460 | 23.3 | 175 | 7500 |
| Fourth | 1.090 | 31.2 | 234 | 7500 |
| Fifth | 0.860 | 3.96 | 273 | 6900 |
| Final drive | | | | 3.56 |

## SUSPENSION

| | |
|---|---|
| Front | independent by unequal length control arms, coil springs & anti-roll bar |
| Rear | independent by unequal length control arms, coil springs & anti-roll bar |
| Wheels | alloy, 7.5J x 17 front |
| | 9.0J x 17 rear |
| Tyres | Pirelli P700 |
| | 215/50ZR 17 front |
| | 255/45ZR 17 rear |

## DIMENSION

| | |
|---|---|
| Wheelbase | 2450mm |
| Front track | 1483mm |
| Rear track | 1577mm |
| Overall length | 4230mm |
| Overall width | 1894mm |
| Overall height | 1170mm |
| Ground clearance | 125mm |
| Kerb weight | 1393kg |
| Weight to power | 6.3 kg/KW |
| Fuel tank | 91.0 litres |

## ACCELERATION

| | |
|---|---|
| 0-100 km/h | 5.60 seconds |
| Standing 400m | n/a |
| Terminal speed (400m) | n/a |

*The above are averages of runs in opposite directions*

| | |
|---|---|
| Standing 400m, best | n/a |
| Terminal speed (400m), best | n/a |

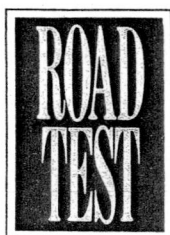

# Ferrari 348tb

Suddenly, the doyen of sports car makers is under fire. [
answer is a car with nothing to prove but a lot to lose

---

**Price as tested** *£67,849* **Top Speed** *163mph* **0-60** *5.6secs* **MPG** *18.4*

---

**For** *Fantastic engine, grip, suspension control, brakes, presence*
**Against** *Sudden oversteer, seats/ride comfort, too noisy*

FERRARI KNOWS A CHARISMATIC badge on a beautiful nose is no longer enough to keep selling cars. Not when confronted by the Japanese challenge from Honda's superb NSX and Nissan's supercar bargain, the new 300ZX. Nor Porsche's Carrera 2, the rejuvenated 911. Basic excellence, backed by continuous development — these were the raw essentials crucial to finding a replacement for the exquisite, if ageing, 328.

But Maranello perfectly understands its clients and the new 348 — a mini Testarossa in appearance and almost as quick — is a predictable successor to the 328, the most popular model in Ferrari's history. It is no less exciting for that.

This may well be Ferrari's best combination of inspiration and practical road ability. In the 348, Ferrari has a roomier and more functional mid-engined coupe, yet one retaining traditional features — and therefore character. This character merges so effectively with Pinin-

farina's latest expression of the Ferrari theme that there's a queue five years long if you order the £67,499.25 car today.

Yet opinion is divided over the styling. Nobody denies the car's basic beauty but there's a question mark on the tacky plastic slats over the rear lights, the ugly and unnecessary strakes along the body's flanks and even the phony, blanked-off grille that's intended to revive memories of bygone racing Ferraris. They're a superfluous distraction from the purity of the 348's seminal shape.

There are no pretensions to the 348 being anything but a two-seater — the two-plus-two role is left to the £7000 cheaper, but essentially mechanically identical, Mondial t — despite a 4ins increase in wheelbase over the 328. Overall length is down by an inch so the overhangs, especially at the rear, have been substantially reduced. Width has grown by an intimidating 5.3ins to 74.5ins. A Carrera 2 is nearly 10ins narrower.

Apart from having its now 3.4-litre quad cam V8 engine mounted longitudinally, the 348 follows established mid-engined Ferrari practice with double wishbone suspension at both ends, huge four-wheel disc brakes, now with an ATE anti-lock device, and driving through the rear wheels only.

Ferrari continues to build the 348 in both cat and non-cat versions, the UK being one of the last markets to get the 'dirty' engine. Ferrari says production of the non-cat engines finishes in October and despite official claims that there's no power loss, the latest figures from Italy indicate catalysed engines suffer a drop of 5bhp and 4lb ft. Verification comes via the gearing. Cat cars get a 3.5625 final drive ratio, the non-cat engine can pull a marginally taller 3.4375 diff. These early British-spec 348s will surely be the most desirable of all, at least until the LM version arrives.

The 348 follows the 328 in offering two body styles, the tb tested here, and the £69,498.81 ▶

ts targa, expected to be the most popular model. Honda's NSX will carry a £60,000 price tag that's undoubtedly been deliberately set in parallel with the 348. Suddenly the £45,821 Porsche asks for the Carrera 2 seems like value for money, while the 300ZX is half the price of the Ferrari.

Ferrari will build around 2500 348s in 1990. It's this exclusivity and those looks plus, as one slightly cynical tester put it, "simply being a Ferrari" that underwrites the 348's success.

## PERFORMANCE AND ECONOMY

This is an extraordinary engine, immensely tractable — it will accept full throttle in fifth gear at idle speed and still feel punchy — and flexible, yet the figures we achieved are slightly disappointing. An extra 30bhp over the 328 has been cancelled out by taller gearing and extra weight so that it is only in the upper reaches, when the slippery shape assists, that the 348 begins to display its superiority.

Still, 5.6secs to 60mph, 0.1secs slower than the 328 and 0.5secs behind the Carrera 2, is swift, if not explosive. It's the standing quarter mile time of 13.8secs, 0.3secs quicker than the old Ferrari and only beaten by the Porsche by 0.1secs, that is a more pertinent criterion of the 348's accelerative ability.

Even with massive 255/45ZR17 Bridgestone RE71s and a 40 per cent limited slip differential, it's possible to leave two long black lines on the bitumen if you drop the clutch with 4500rpm or more on the tachometer. Firm in weight, the clutch is like so many of the Ferrari's controls in divulging real feel through a smooth and progressive action that allows the

driver to regulate exactly the degree of wheelspin. Even without breaking adhesion the 348 slips away smoothly, quickly, on minute throttle openings, encouraged by a Ferrari engine with what not so long ago would have been regarded as an inconceivably mild nature at low revs.

Squeeze down on the throttle and you'll discover its travel is actually quite long, and the first impressions of low gearing created by the engine noise quite erroneous. What makes the Ferrari so exhilarating to drive is the sheer dimension of its rev range.

There's punch from as low as the 1000rpm

idle and then a long seamless pull through veritable symphony of disparate sounds all th way to the 7500rpm red line, even the 7800rp cut-out. Always responsive, you tend t change up at around 4000rpm in norma driving, leaving most other cars in your wake knowing you've used only half the rev rang and knowing, too, that if you push harder ju as the exhaust note is transformed abov 5000rpm, so the engine becomes even mor vibrant, full of fire and fight.

Only two cars in our hands have gone faste than the 348 in the UK: Ferrari's 171mp Testarossa and Porsche's 165mph 928G'

**Grip from RE71 Bridgestones is excellent. 348 goes exactly where it is pointed, with mildest hint of understeer. At the limit, it snaps into oversteer slide**

Even at a best speed of 164mph — which translates to over 170mph on a suitable piece of straight autobahn — around the Millbrook high speed bowl the 348 felt secure. Despite the wheel twitching continuously, the Ferrari displayed greater stability than the Carrera 2 or 4, and felt far superior to the recently tested and slower Aston Martin Virage or Nissan 300ZX. The factory claims a top speed of 171mph, or 7300rpm, a mere 100rpm above the point of peak power and therefore entirely feasible.

Why then does Ferrari feel the need to fit a speedometer that is so optimistic? At an indicated 50mph the car is travelling at 43mph,

at 100mph it's doing a true 90mph.

Crack open a window an inch or two and the sound of the V8 engine will be music to a Ferraristi's ears, from the slight V8 throb at low revs, through a period of comparative calm when gear whine approaches the exhaust note and then, from 5000rpm onwards, a feverish blend of howling cams, visceral induction roar and bellowing exhaust. Many drivers, however, will surely spend more time with the windows closed. In this condition the engine is merely tiringly noisy, emitting an uninteresting, whining sound that's rivaled by excessive tyre noise and wind roar around the frameless

door glass. It's a combination to make motorway driving exhausting.

One of the most important tactile ingredients that makes a Ferrari a Ferrari is the thin chrome gearlever jutting out of the open chrome gate. Improved synchronisers mean the change is lighter and quicker than the 328's, if never as slick as a Carrera 2's. There's still an initial stiffness as the lever is moved out of one ratio into neutral, then mild resistance before it slips into the next gear. During our time with the car this inclination to obstinacy grew more marked and the heavy spring loading to the second/third plane (first is down on a dog-leg opposite reverse) more obvious. Still, when you hurry the change, the metal-to-metal ring as the lever hits the gate at the end of each shift between the close ratios adds something tangible to its stature.

Given its performance, the 348 is surprisingly frugal. Our hard-driven test car averaged 18.4mpg, 0.1mpg better than the 328, and returned 22.6mpg on one fill, better than the projected touring consumption of 21.4mpg. Which makes the imprecise fuel gauge even less logical than the erroneous speedo. Fill the 20.9-gallon tank when the gauge is reading empty and the warning light aglow, and you'll be lucky to squeeze in 15 gallons, effectively reducing the touring range of 447 miles by a quarter.

## HANDLING AND RIDE
Ferrari's intrinsic philosophy for the 348 is perfectly represented by the steering. There's the weighting — heavy only at low speeds, exactly right everywhere else. And there's the ▶

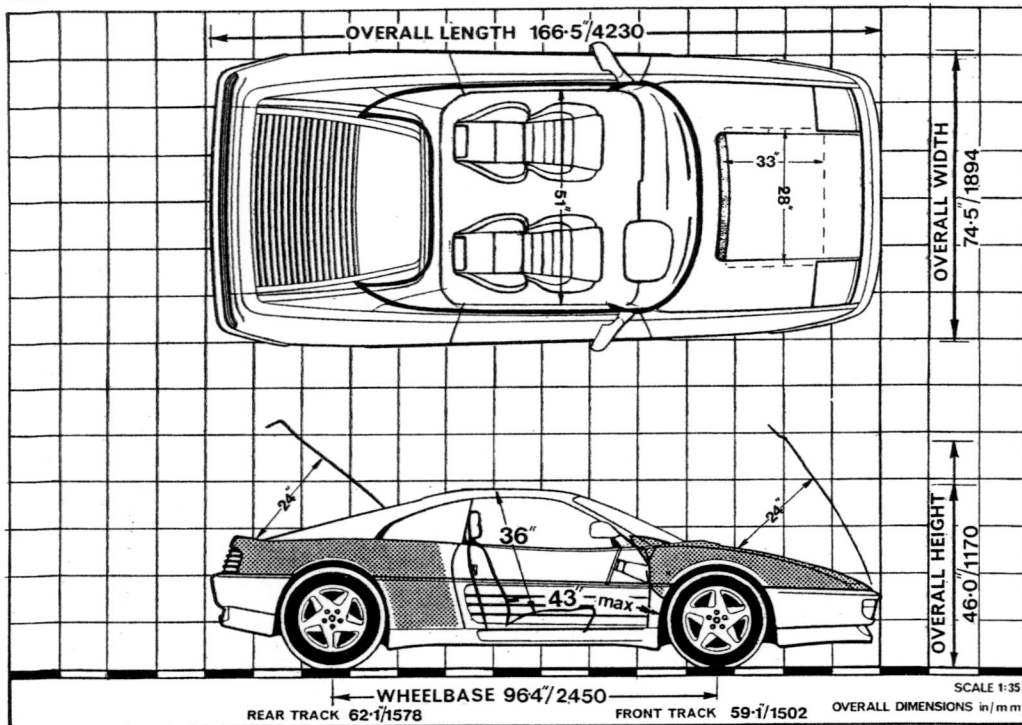

OVERALL LENGTH 166·5/4230
OVERALL WIDTH 74·5/1894
OVERALL HEIGHT 46·0/1170
33"
28"
51"
36"
43" max
24"
24"
WHEELBASE 96·4"/2450
REAR TRACK 62·1/1578
FRONT TRACK 59·1/1502
SCALE 1:35
OVERALL DIMENSIONS in/mm

## PERFORMANCE

### MAXIMUM SPEEDS

| Gear | mph | km/h |
|---|---|---|
| Top (mean) | 163 | 262 |
| (best) | 164 | 263 |
| 4th | 144 | 232 |
| 3rd | 108 | 173 |
| 2nd | 74 | 119 |
| 1st | 48 | 78 |

### ACCELERATION FROM REST

| True mph | Time (secs) | Sp |
|---|---|---|
| 30 | 2.1 | |
| 40 | 3.0 | |
| 50 | 4.4 | |
| 60 | 5.6 | |
| 70 | 7.1 | |
| 80 | 9.0 | |
| 90 | 10.9 | |
| 100 | 13.3 | |
| 110 | 16.7 | |
| 120 | 20.2 | |
| 130 | 24.3 | |

**Standing ¼-mile:** 13.8secs, 100mp
**Standing km:** 25.3secs, 130mph
**30-70mph thro' gears:** 5.0secs

### ACCELERATION IN EACH GEAR

| mph | Top | 4th | 3rd |
|---|---|---|---|
| 10-30 | — | — | 4.8 |
| 20-40 | 8.5 | 6.0 | 4.2 |
| 30-50 | 7.9 | 5.6 | 3.7 |
| 40-60 | 7.7 | 5.4 | 3.6 |
| 50-70 | 7.6 | 5.1 | 3.7 |
| 60-80 | 7.3 | 4.9 | 3.8 |
| 70-90 | 7.2 | 5.2 | 3.8 |
| 80-100 | 8.1 | 5.7 | 4.1 |
| 90-110 | 8.9 | 6.0 | — |
| 100-120 | 9.9 | 6.7 | — |
| 110-130 | 7.9 | | |

### FUEL CONSUMPTION

**Overall mpg:** 18.4 (15.3 litres/100km
**Touring mpg:** 21.4 (13.2 litres/100k
**Govt tests mpg:** 15.9mpg (urban)
36.7mpg (steady 56mph)
28.5mpg (steady 75mph)
**Fuel grade:** Four star (97RM) or unleaded (95RM)
**Tank capacity:** 20.89 galls (95 litres
**Max range*:** 447 miles
* Based on Government fuel economy figures: 50 per cent of urban cycle, 25 cent each of 56/75mph consumptions.

### BRAKING

**Fade** (from 100mph in neutral)
**Pedal load (lb) for 0.5g stops**

| start/end | | start |
|---|---|---|
| 1 | 20-20 | 6 |
| 2 | 15-15 | 7 |
| 3 | 20-20 | 8 |
| 4 | 20-20 | 9 |
| 5 | 20-20 | 10 |

**Response** (from 30mph in neutral)

| Load | g | Distance |
|---|---|---|
| 10lb | 0.25 | 120ft |
| 20lb | 0.45 | 67ft |
| 30lb | 0.65 | 46ft |
| 40lb | 0.90 | 33ft |
| 50lb | 1.0 | 30ft |
| Parking brake | 0.30 | 100ft |

### WEIGHT

**Kerb** 3226lb/1465kg
**Distribution %F/R** 41/59
**Test** 3626lb/1646kg
**Max payload** 3700lbs/1680kgs

### TEST CONDITIONS

| | |
|---|---|
| **Wind** | 9-11 |
| **Temperature** | 17deg C (62de |
| **Barometer** | 1010 |
| **Surface** | dry asphalt/con |
| **Test distance** | 1569 |

Figures taken at 2689 miles by our own staff at the Lotus Group proving groun Millbrook.

All *Autocar & Motor* test results are su to world copyright and may not be reproduced without the Editor's writte permission.

## SPECIFICATION

### ENGINE

Longitudinal, mid, rear-wheel drive.
**Capacity** 3405cc, 8 cylinders in 90 deg V.
**Bore** 85mm. **stroke** 75mm.
**Compression ratio** 10.4 to 1.
**Head/block** al alloy/al alloy.
**Valve gear** dohc, 4 valves per cylinder.
**Ignition and fuel** breaker-less electronic ignition, Bosch Motronic M2.5 fuel injection.
**Max power** 300bhp (PS-DIN) (221kW ISO) at 7200rpm. **Max torque** 238lb ft (323 Nm) at 4200rpm.

### TRANSMISSION

5-speed manual.

| Gear | Ratio | mph/1000rpm |
|---|---|---|
| Top | 0.86 | 23.3 |
| 4th | 1.09 | 18.5 |
| 3rd | 1.46 | 13.8 |
| 2nd | 2.11 | 9.5 |
| 1st | 3.21 | 6.2 |

Final drive ratio 3.44 to 1. Limited slip differential.

### SUSPENSION

**Front,** independent, double wishbone, coil springs, telescopic dampers, anti-roll bar.
**Rear,** double wishbone, telescopic dampers, anti-roll bar.

### STEERING

Rack and pinion, 3.2 turns lock to lock.

### BRAKES

**Front** 11.8ins (299mm) dia ventilated disc.
**Rear** 12.25ins (311mm) dia ventilated disc.

### WHEELS AND TYRES

Cast alloy 7.5ins rims front, 9ins rims rear, 215/50ZR17 front, Bridgestone tyres 255/45ZR17 rear.

### SOLD IN THE UK BY

Maranello Concessionaires Ltd
Thorpe Industrial Estate
Egham, Surrey, UK
TW20 8RJ
Tel: (0784) 436222

## COSTS

| | |
|---|---|
| **Total** (in UK) | £67,499 |
| **Delivery, road tax, plates** | £350 |
| **On the road price** | £67,849 |
| **Options fitted to test car:** | None |
| **Total as tested** | £67,849 |

### SERVICE

Major service 12,000 miles — service time n/a hrs. Intermediate service 6,000 miles — service time n/a hrs. Oil change 6,000 miles — service time n/a hrs.

### PARTS COST (Inc VAT)

| | |
|---|---|
| Oil filter | £8.74 |
| Air filter | £15.99 |
| Spark plugs (set) | £61.27 |
| Brake pads (2 wheels) front | £161.08 |
| Brake pads (2 wheels) rear | £161.08 |
| Exhaust complete | £1879.74 |
| Tyre — each (typical) F/R £172.50/£228.75 | |
| Windscreen | £421.85 |
| Headlamp unit | £184.57 |
| Front wing | £446.67 |
| Rear bumper | £1535.43 |

### WARRANTY

12 months/unlimited mileage, 1 year anti-corrosion, 12 months breakdown recovery renewable.

## EQUIPMENT

| | |
|---|---|
| Anti-lock brakes | ● |
| Self-levelling suspension | — |
| Alloy wheels | ● |
| Auto gearbox | — |
| Power-assisted steering | — |
| Limited slip differential | ● |
| Steering rake | ● |
| Seat height adjustment | — |
| Electric seat adjustment | — |
| Lumbar adjustment | — |
| Head restraints | ● |
| Intermittent wipe | ● |
| Heated seats | — |
| Leather trim | ● |
| Air conditioning | ● |
| Cruise control | — |
| Radio/cassette player | £837.20 |
| Electric aerial | — |
| 4 speakers | ● |
| Electric windows F | ● |
| Central locking | — |
| Front fog/driving lamps | ● |
| Headlamp wash wipe | — |
| Electric tilt/slide sunroof | — |
| Metallic paint | no cost option |

● Standard — Not available

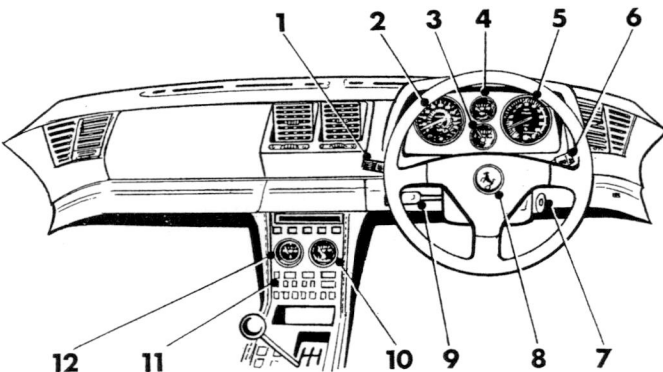

**1** Lights. **2** Speedometer. **3** Temperature gauge. **4** Oil pressure gauge. **5** Revcounter. **6** Windscreen wash/wipe. **7** Ignition/steering lock. **8** Horn. **9** Indicators. **10** Fuel gauge. **11** Air-conditioning controls. **12** Oil temperature gauge.

gearing, with an agile 3.2 turns even if they are over an obese 39.5ft turning circle. Plus of course there's the steering's feel — a subtlety of communication that portrays even a change of road surface. The combination of all this makes for steering that's simply perfect for such a car. Kick-back over ridges or ruts, too often the penalty for such preciseness, is but a mild tremor.

Combine this with brilliant suspension control, the kind of composure that keeps the body flat, even over undulating minor roads or when accelerating and braking at the limit, and you have a car that turns into corners at immense speeds without altering its attitude. You can flick the 348 through a series of tight corners knowing the Ferrari's stance is a constant, feeling the steering load varying discreetly — building up steadily towards the apex of a corner — and measuring the g-forces by the body's strain against the heavily bolstered sides of the seat. The Ferrari driver always retains an uninterrupted link with the road. It's a vital factor in the 348's fascination.

Given the immense grip of the excellent RE71 Bridgestone tyres on both dry and wet roads you'd expect the Ferrari to handle well, with very high limits of adhesion. High-speed stability is excellent, traction out of tight corners exemplary. So in essence the 348 goes exactly where it is pointed with just a touch of steady understeer.

Up to a point. Then, when the car is travelling exceptionally quickly, the driver's seat-of-the-pants feel will need to be susceptible to the smallest change in steering feel and weight transfer. Ferrari will tell you the 348 is a more progressive handling car than the 328. Perhaps, but there is only a small band of progressive chassis behaviour before the car snaps into an oversteer slide that almost inevitably will end in a 180deg spin.

Experience indicates any analysis of the 348's ride will invariably be split between the two extremes of normal commuter/motorway driving and cross-country work. Unable to exploit the 348's full performance, handling and steering potential, a driver discovers a ride firm to the point of being bad, transferring every change in road surface to the car's occupants, sometimes verging on harshness. On the other hand, the driver who has access to roads capable of testing every facet of the Ferrari's performance will enjoy this tautness of control and relish the precision of the suspension. When working very hard, the suspension has an ability to absorb humps and changes in camber without so much as a shiver.

Nobody doubted the 348's brakes. For a fleeting instant the pedal feels dead, then over a very short, yet progressive, travel it becomes immensely powerful.

## AT THE WHEEL
Simply but boldly styled, the 348's cabin is, with a couple of exceptions, superbly finished, though the white leather trim would quickly become grubby. Our dislikes are the stiff black door handles and cheap-looking lid to the central console. A small binnacle just in front of the small, almost vertically-mounted leather-bound and perfectly sized steering wheel contains 200mph speedometer and 10,000rpm revcounter, which are split by oil pressure and water temperature gauges. Average-sized drivers can lower the wheel to an ideal position but they will find the top of the steering wheel blocks their view of the top half of both major

dials and all of the oil pressure gauge. The fuel and oil temperature gauges are mounted too low on the central console, just above pushbutton controls for the air conditioning. Drivers up to 6ft tall will find the driving position close to perfect, while those over 6ft will welcome the extra room over the 328 even if the driving position is still rather knees-up.

## COMFORT AND SPACE
Indeed, tall drivers will wish for even more rearward travel for the heavily bolstered bucket seat. The left leg can be stretched out, but only by slipping it under the clutch pedal.

Brake and accelerator are perfectly positioned to make heel-and-toe changes, using the ball of the foot, routine. The pedals are offset slightly to the left, something noticed the first time but then discounted.

Seat adjustment is limited to reach and rake, and with no cushion height or tilt adjustment under-thigh support is very poor for the long legged. This low and flat cushion, and a lack of lumbar support, encourages the driver to slump — with an aching backside the result even on a journey of an hour.

There's certainly more room than the 328 offered and visibility is impressive for a ▶

**Seats encourage you to slump but offer good side support. Leather height-adjustable wheel can block out view of half of major dials and all of oil pressure gauge**

Longitudinally-mounted 3.4-litre V8 puts out 238lb ft of torque at 4200rpm and 300bhp at 7200. Engine will rev until 7800rpm cut-out

◀ mid-engined car, though the driver sees little of the bonnet and needs to raise the headlights to have any indication of where the prow begins. You don't expect entry and exit to be easy on a car as low as the 348, but the position of the steering wheel and the intrusion of the front wheelarch mean it's a laborious exercise. The boot, under the nose, is far deeper than you expect because there's no spare wheel. Just as well because the glovebox is tiny and there are no door bins.

### FINISH AND EQUIPMENT

For the most part beautifully put together, the 348 feels more rigid than any previous Ferrari. It's now almost Porsche-like in this regard. The doors close with a similar, comforting, secure sound. The test car did develop a mild resonance from a loose component in the engine bay but, this aside, gave no cause to doubt its long-term durability.

Central locking, air conditioning, anti-lock brakes, a leather interior, electric windows, aerial and speakers — but not the stereo unit — are standard.

### VERDICT

There are few surprises in the 348, and we suspect most Ferrari owners wouldn't have it any other way. This car has a passion and an energy matched by few others, a charisma that is peerless. Yet it is badly flawed in some areas: the seats, the ride and the noise levels unite to make it unsuitable for long motorway journeys. This Ferrari would not be a soothing companion on a swift Continental trip. Accept that compromise, understand it means that

Ferrari's propensity for building a car for ultimate enjoyment in two hour bursts hasn't changed, and the 348 is a joy.

Even so, those who have driven the Honda NSX wondered if the Ferrari represents the old school of mid-engine chassis design. They would wish for more neutral and progressive ultimate handling, while accepting that few drivers will approach the 348's limits on public roads. The Ferrari faithful, forgetting the 348's unhappy demeanour on the highway, will sing its praises as an object of great beauty and pure driving pleasure. Ferrari asserts that this is enough; Honda would suggest it's not. ■

### SUMMARY

| | |
|---|---|
| Performance | ★★★★★★★★☆☆ |
| Economy | ★★★★★★★☆☆☆ |
| Transmission | ★★★★★★★☆☆☆ |
| Handling | ★★★★★★★☆☆☆ |
| Ride comfort | ★★★☆☆☆☆☆☆☆ |
| Brakes | ★★★★★★★★★★ |
| Accommodation | ★★★★★★☆☆☆☆ |
| Boot/storage | ★★★★★★☆☆☆☆ |
| At the wheel | ★★★★★☆☆☆☆☆ |
| Visibility | ★★★★★★☆☆☆☆ |
| Instruments | ★★★★★☆☆☆☆☆ |
| Heating | ★★★★★★☆☆☆☆ |
| Ventilation | ★★★★★★★★☆☆ |
| Noise | ★★☆☆☆☆☆☆☆☆ |
| Finish | ★★★★★★★★★☆ |
| Equipment | ★★★★★★★★☆☆ |
| **OUR RATING** | ★★★★★★★★☆☆ |
| **VALUE RATING** | ★★★★★★★☆☆☆ |

### TECHNICAL FOCUS

*The 348's major change over the 328 is the adoption of a **longitudinal layout** for th larger capacity V8 engine, first seen on the Mondial t. Locating the mid-mounted engin this way means it has been possible to lower powerplant by 5ins, with benefits to roadho and handling, and serviceability. The geart now sits at the end of the engine, rather than beneath it, drive coming from the engine via 90deg bevel gear set to the hydraulically-operated clutch. This is mounted with the flywheel in an external housing at the end of drivetrain, rather than being on the end of t crankshaft.*

*A 40 per cent limited slip differential is coupled to the five-speed gearbox by cylindr transfer gears.*

*Interestingly the unleaded engines, which Ferrari says have the same 300bhp at 7200 and 238lb ft of torque at 4200rpm as the lea versions still sold in the UK, get slightly lou gearing via a 3.5625 final drive compared t 3.4375 for the non-cat cars. The old Bosch K-Jetronic injection has been replaced by th latest **Motronic M2.5 system**, said to m fuel more effectively.*

*The only engine change over the Mondial the lack of a power steering pump, Ferrari resolving that it's small sports car should ret direct link, via manual rack and pinion stee between road and driver.*

*Styling is all-new, and Pininfarina has c the drag co-efficient from 0.36 to 0.32. Ferr decision to move the radiators from the nose beside the engine helps account for the massi 5.3ins increase in width. The 74.5ins 348 is nearly 10ins wider than a Carrera 2.*

*If the 348 feels more solid than the old 32 that's hardly surprising, since Ferrari claim **torsional rigidity** of the tb is improved b per cent (the ts targa is only five per cent bett than the old 328; reason enough to stick wit coupe body).*

*This is achieved through the use of a self-supporting chassis frame to which is bolt tubular box section at the rear supporting the engine and transaxle.*

*Ferrari has stuck with the 328's basic suspension layout of double wishbones, coil springs and anti-roll bars front and rear. Th **wishbones** are of a new stamped steel desi while the hub carriers are now forged to redu unsprung weight. The cast aluminium wheels have gone up an inch in diameter and wider, lower profile Bridgestone RE17 tyres*